T0368633

But Then

She Smiled

Daily Dose of Positive Affirmations:
A Yearlong Journey of Empowerment and Inspiration

ANNISE

To order additional copies of this book, contact:
Xlibris
844-714-8691
www.Xlibris.com
Orders@Xlibris.com

ISBN: Softcover   979-8-3694-3393-5
         Hardcover   979-8-3694-3404-8
         EBook   979-8-3694-3392-8

Library of Congress Control Number: 2024923869

Print information available on the last page

Rev. date: 11/27/2024

Contents

Dedication

To Henneh (1965–1992) and Jemi (1960–2020), my beloved siblings, with all my love. Though you left us too soon, your light continues to shine in my heart. This is for you, and for the legacy of love and strength you've left behind.

Preface

Hello, dear friend. Though we may not know each other personally, there's something I'm sure we share—the challenges life throws at us and the daily battle to stay positive in the midst of it all.

Like many of you, I've faced my share of struggles growing up—some visible, some hidden deep within. But even as a young girl, I made a conscious decision to seek the good in every situation, no matter how difficult or complicated it seemed. This mindset, while not always easy, became my compass. It helped me navigate through tough times, difficult relationships, and moments where hope seemed elusive. Now, as an adult, I continue to rely on this internal compass to guide me—whether I'm dealing with challenges in my career, personal life, or emotional health. Life, after all, will always have its obstacles, but it is how we respond to them that shapes who we are and the joy we carry within us.

I've always believed that while we cannot control every circumstance, we have the power to choose how we react. Now that was a challenge for me and one that I really had to work on because I am naturally a reactive person. However, my desire for peace and happiness has helped me contain that emotionally reactive side. Writing and sharing daily positive and uplifting affirmations has contributed towards that journey and goal and that was one of my biggest inspirations for writing this book—to help others find their happiness despite challenges.

Happiness, for me, is something we can create even when it feels far away. When life has tried to knock me down, I've made it a habit to smile, even in situations when crying seems like the natural thing to do. I have trained my mind to become my own I've learned to transform my struggles into opportunities to lift others, turning pain into purpose and choosing to find light, even in the darkest corners. I have trained my mind to become my own cheerleader in the darkest hours while positive affirmations have been my lifeline to keep my soul buoyant. For me, positivity isn't just a mindset—it's a survival tool.

Raised by a strong single mother, my mama worked hard to raise her own six biological kids and plenty others, and this became increasingly challenging after my father checked out. While the absence of my father left invisible scars, it also pushed me to become stronger and more resilient. I learned the power of independence and perseverance from my mother, and it's those lessons that continue to guide me today.

Over time, life has tested me in many ways – through the highs and lows of marriage and the painful process of divorce, the heartache of broken friendships that I once thought would last a lifetime, and the struggles of balancing personal and professional challenges. I've faced moments of doubt and uncertainty, where the road ahead seemed unclear and the weight of expectations felt too heavy to carry. From career setbacks to personal disappointments, life has been an unpredictable journey that has often pushed me beyond my comfort zone. Yet, with each test, I have learned invaluable lessons about resilience, self-worth, and the importance of surrounding myself with those who uplift and support me. These experiences, though painful, have shaped me into the person I am today—stronger, more self-aware, and more determined to live authentically.

Through it all, I have learned that life is not about perfection or avoiding hardship, but about how we rise from our setbacks, mend what's broken, and continue forward with hope. Each trial has been a teacher, showing me the power of forgiveness, the necessity of letting go, and the importance of nurturing the connections that truly matter. But for all the challenges I had faced, I was never prepared for death.

One of the most painful moments came when we lost my brother, Henneh, in a tragic drowning accident. It's a day forever etched into my soul. That day was one of the darkest days of my life. Our grief as a family was unbearable, but I did what I always do—put on a brave face. I dug deep into my sense of humor, the side of me that has always been my way of coping, and used it to help my siblings get through our grief. My mother, though, retreated into silence. She didn't speak much for nearly a year; she just stared into space, her heart clearly shattered.

Tragedy struck again in 2020 when we suddenly lost my sister, Jemi. The pain of losing someone so dear so suddenly is unimaginable and sometimes, even unmanageable—I will not wish it on my worst enemy. It was a shock that none of us were prepared for. The doctors said it was an aortic dissection, but I believe it was the weight of the world that took her—her heart was too full of love for this cruel earth. After ten hours of surgery and two days on life support, we were forced to make the hardest decision of our life—turn that machine off.

We were broken. Jemi left behind her only daughter, Karina, who she loved with every fiber of her being. Our hearts remain shattered to this day and our lives are forever changed. There are no words to describe such a pain or a way to fill such a void. The world as we knew it changed forever, and to this day, not a moment goes by when I don't feel her absence. I still cry every day. This pain is something you can't describe, and I hope you never have to experience it. Losing someone you love so suddenly is like losing the air you breathe. Nothing is the same.

During this period of grief, I turned to what I knew best—lifting others, finding humor in the sadness, and creating light even in the darkest times. I found ways to create laughter and invoke happier memories. I would try to recount a funny story of our childhood or think about happy moments to ease the pain. This is the only way I know to survive such pain or to help others. While I do recognize the seriousness of what was happening, I also understood that I had to step up and create a space for laughter. Do not feel guilty if you want to return to some of your normal activities during your mourning period because that is part of your healing. I've come to realize that kindness, grace, and positivity are not only ways to connect with others but also ways to heal ourselves. In uplifting others, I often find my own strength.

So the following is my message to you, friend: Always seek the light in the darkness. There will be times when it feels impossible, and it is those times that you will need to dig deep into your survival tool kit. I believe that there is always something to be learned from every experience, even the painful ones. As long as we're alive, there will always be a lesson to discover and a reason to smile.

Acknowledgments

To my three beloved children—Rashawn, my oldest, the first human who taught me the art of stillness, and a man of few words, yet your presence speaks volumes; Shania, my only daughter, my best friend – "you will forever be the most beautiful girl in the world." In you, I see myself, and that alone is enough. You push me beyond heights I could never have imagined, and your support is unwavering. The best advice you ever gave me was that I should start "giving others the same energy they give me." That changed how I viewed the world in that very instant; and Shane, my last joy "How could my own baby teach me so much about life while challenging me so deeply?" ♥ ♥ ♥

To my husband, Edward, thank you for taking a leap across the pond in the name of love. I can't tell you how many times I've had to whisper affirmations in front of the mirror when you drive me crazy—but they did say, "Love will make you crazy." Thank you from my heart for your support on this journey.

To Mama Clara, my mother, my rock, the strongest woman I know. To know you is to love you. Your strength is unshakable, your faith unbreakable. Your holy oil seems to solve all of life's mysteries, and your laughter makes the world lighter. You are a true blessing.

To my sisters, Lilah and Soriah, my wombmates—what would my life be without you two? Quieter, no doubt, but infinitely less vibrant. When the world feels heavy, I know I can count on you both to be there, ready to lift me up and carry me through. We started as four, and now we are three. Jemi, you will always be a part of us even though you are gone too soon.

To Fatou, for your endless kindness, showing us that some humans are as close to perfection as they get.

To my soul sisters: Jules, Katie, Herbertina, Saddah, Okokie, Naasu, Laura, Mia, Renous, and Jita; my allies: Bintou H, Lucy, ZZ, and Jugu; and to my kindred spirits: Sana and Yabome: I am deeply grateful for each of you. At some point, we have navigated through some tidal waves together, shared laughter and tears but in the midst of it all, your unwavering encouragement has enriched my life immensely – I love you all for that.

My surrogate mothers: Linda Jones, Sylvia Turner and Ann-Marie Akpan - thank you for always loving me and all your prayers.

My dearest A, no time or distance has ever come between us. Your honest feedback and tender approach to life remain unmatched. You have a way of cutting through the noise with a calmness that will steady anyone. I am forever grateful for your friendship and support.

To all my nieces, nephews, bonus siblings and in-laws—I thank you all for the love and support.

To my Convent Sisters and the Mid-Atlantic Chapter, I hope you find something in this book that uplifts your soul, empowers your spirit, inspires you somehow, and strengthens our sisterhood. Thank you for allowing me to lead and learn, for teaching me patience, for showing me how our differences are also our strengths, and for helping me understand my purpose. I bet you didn't even know this, but you have given me the courage to be more intentional and non-judgmental. Let us continue to give and lead with kindness.

Al Fitchett, thank you for being my mentor and office "dad." You truly looked out for me, always urging me to never accept less and reminding me I was destined for more. I may not have made it big yet, but I did write that book, and hopefully, it's just the beginning!

Pastor Fifi, this book might not have happened without you. Earlier this year, you called me, saying God led you to encourage me to write a book. You promised to pray for me, knowing it would be my mission. Your prayers have been answered— the year is up, and here we are!

To all the friends I've loved and lost—I thank you for the lessons. You unknowingly taught me resilience, self-care, and how to find light through the cracks in the dark. Our journey may have ended, but love remains. Only a fool holds a grudge instead of keeping love and drawing boundaries.

I would like to extend my heartfelt gratitude to the incredible team of editors and photographers who have brought this book to life. A special shout-out to Jules for your invaluable editorial support and for your daily push that kept me moving forward, ensuring this book reached its completion. Your dedication has been truly appreciated.

To you reading this book right now, I thank you so deeply from my heart for your support. I hope this book uplifts and inspires you in some way. Remember that your smile is contagious so take it everywhere.

And finally, to all my teachers and everyone who has been part of this wild ride of life—be it a negative or positive connection, whether you cheered me on from the sidelines or gave me the occasional push when I needed it—thank you. You've all shaped me in ways big and small, some of which I'm still discovering (and will likely need therapy for later, but that's a different story and probably another book). I may not have all the answers, but I do know this—you have all in your own ways inspired me in some form to garner up the courage to do this and sometimes, unintentionally contributed toward this little book of mine. So from the bottom of my heart (and the top of my ever-growing to-do list), thank you.

Here's to many more books—both literal and figurative!

Introduction

But Then She Smiled, Daily Dose of Positive Affirmations: A Yearlong Journey of Empowerment and Inspiration is designed to guide you through a transformative journey of personal growth, self-compassion, and positivity. As we navigate life, it's easy to become overwhelmed by the pressures of everyday responsibilities, self-doubt, and negativity.

This book aims to combat those challenges by providing you with daily affirmations that inspire you to reclaim your power, stay grounded, and embrace your true potential. The idea behind this was to uplift and empower you daily and also to remind you to stay positive in the midst of chaos or self-doubt.

Why affirmations? Our thoughts shape our reality, and by cultivating positive and intentional thinking, we set the foundation for a life filled with purpose, joy, and fulfillment. Affirmations are powerful tools that remind us of our inner strength, shifting our mindset from doubt to confidence, from fear to courage, and from self-criticism to self-love. This book will serve as your companion and compass throughout the year, encouraging you to focus on what truly matters and to make each day an opportunity for growth and empowerment. It is meant to force you to focus on the good and only see the lessons in everything else. One never fails if one learns a lesson in every situation regardless of the outcome.

Each month in this book focuses on a different theme, from manifesting new beginnings in January to embracing gratitude and compassion in December. Each chapter builds upon the previous one, creating a holistic approach to self-development. These themes have been chosen to help you grow in all areas of life—mentally, emotionally, and spiritually. Be intentional about your inner peace and self-growth and allow this book to help you along the way.

As you embark on this year-long journey, remember that growth takes time. Some days will be harder than others, but each day is an opportunity to reset, refocus, and make progress toward your goals. Be gentle with yourself, trust the process, and stay committed to your personal journey.

Let this book be a source of encouragement, hope, and inspiration. Whether you're looking to overcome self-doubt, build confidence, or simply find more joy in everyday moments, these affirmations will support you every step of the way. Here's to a year of positive transformation, and to creating the life you truly deserve.

I hope sharing some of my own personal struggles and challenges and how viewing them from an angle of positivity and not wallowing in self-pity will empower and inspire you to learn to face your challenges as lessons and strive to smile amid the chaos.

Manifesting New Beginnings and Positive Change

The start of a new year brings with it a powerful invitation—a fresh slate, a chance to reset, refocus, and welcome positive change into every aspect of your life. It's a time when we're naturally motivated to let go of old habits, mindsets, and patterns that no longer serve us, replacing them with new, purposeful ways of thinking and living. This is the essence of growth—letting go of what's holding you back and stepping into what will propel you forward.

However, remember that transformation will not occur overnight. Growth is a gradual process, requiring both patience and perseverance. The challenges you wish to overcome don't arise in a single day, so it's important to allow yourself the same grace as you work to overcome them. Each small step forward, each misstep corrected, and each lesson learned is a building block to something more aligned with your highest potential.

Change often requires us to learn from our mistakes. It encourages us to see each setback not as a failure but as a vital part of the journey. Mistakes reveal the areas in our lives that need adjustment and clarity, helping us make more intentional choices along the way. This month, give yourself the freedom to experiment, to fall, and to get back up with more insight than before.

As you embark on this path of transformation, trust the process. Set realistic expectations, knowing that while the road may be long, every day brings you closer to the life you envision. Let this be a time to focus on what truly matters, building habits that nurture growth and shedding anything that distracts from your purpose. With consistent effort and belief, the positive changes you seek will gradually manifest, creating a foundation for a brighter, more fulfilling year ahead.

Personal Reflection: The Courage to Start Over

There's something undeniably magical about a new year. It's not merely the change of date but the opportunity it offers to start fresh. Each January, I'm reminded that no matter how challenging the previous year was, we're given another chance to rewrite our story. Starting over doesn't erase the past; it builds upon it—the lessons we've learned, the strength we've gained, and the wisdom we've gathered along the way. We are all in a constant state of becoming.

There have been times in my life when change felt daunting or when stepping away from the comfort of the familiar felt terrifying. Whether it was a career shift, a painful loss, or a simple decision to show up differently for myself, change has always arrived hand in hand with hesitation. But I've learned that embracing new beginnings is less about chasing perfection and more about summoning courage. It's about daring to take that first step, even if you're uncertain about the outcome.

You don't need to wait for the start of a new year to make a change or for a new age. One of the biggest changes I have ever made in my adult life was choosing to end my marriage of almost twenty years. Despite how much we had grown apart, marriage felt safe, even when the fire was gone. But some changes are necessary. I remember the ache in my throat as I held back tears the day I said goodbye to my ex-husband.

He had just loaded the last box onto the moving truck. We hugged, both heartbroken that our "'til death do us part" had ended. We were good people after all, but somehow, along the way, our dreams and plans had unraveled. The sold sign on our front yard was a solemn reminder that this chapter was closing. We had poured our hearts into that beautiful six-bedroom home, believing it would be our forever home but yet, something essential was missing. So here we were.

As I drove the moving truck to my new home with my three kids, aged fifteen, fourteen, and ten, I choked up. I wasn't overly worried about raising my daughter as a single mom, but the thought of raising two boys alone filled me with doubt. Yet somehow, I did it—we did it. The one thing my ex-husband and I got right was our commitment to co-parenting.

I had no choice now. The house had been sold, I had signed a new lease for a townhome in our same community so the kids could keep going to the same schools, and now I had to deal with the change.

I stepped into my new life as a single mom and a renter, a word I struggled with. The idea of renting depressed me because I had always been a homeowner and that signified stability to me. It was too late now. I had made my choices. The music of life was playing, and I could either join in or stand on the sidelines. There's no joy in standing still, so I chose to dance, awkward and uncertain but moving forward.

The following years were a whirlwind. I had to balance sports, school events, and three growing kids; focus on my career; go back to school for my MBA; and attempt to date again—dating, OMG, dating! That was challenging. It was just a very weird place to be. I only knew how to be a parent and a wife. One night, in a fit of frustration over something as simple as the dishes, I completely lost it with my kids. They had never talked back before, but they were angry, and they took it all out on me. That night, I questioned everything. I locked myself in my bathroom, allowing the weight of my struggles to wash over me.

In moments like those, I turn to my pen and the shower—my best friends, knowing all my secrets. They help me release my pain in private so that I can face the world anew. And when I'm done, I do what I know best—I stand tall, square my shoulders, straighten my back, and smile.

A couple of years later, I was starting to get used to my new lifestyle. Heck, I even got brave and taught my daughter to drive. Now if you know me at all, this would make you chuckle. Teaching Nia to drive was a recipe for a heart attack. I am not sure why I opted to punish myself and took on that assignment. Maybe, it was part of our bonding and healing period, but boy did we have some screaming matches during those lessons. I am still not sure it was a good idea but hey, she did pass her driving test and has been driving for the last ten years without even hitting a deer, so I think we did alright.

We definitely got a lot of things right but also had a few horrible days. Like the time Shane decided to run away. It was dead in the winter and after a few hours, we realized Shane was not in the house. Rashawn and Nia checked in with his friends in the neighborhood, but no one had seen him and fear began to set in. The more doors we knocked on, the more scared I became. My heart started pounding and suddenly, I was thinking the worst. What if we never find him? I had seen parents on TV begging for their lost kids to return home safely. I did not want to be one of those heartbroken parents. My mind was way ahead of me and not in a good way.

I jumped in my van. We had a six-seater Nissan Quest at the time, which was perfect for a soccer mom. I had no idea where I was driving to at this point, and then my instinct told me to check at our old home we had recently moved out of because I remembered how sad Shane was to move away, and some days, he would randomly ask me if I could buy that same house again. I knew he missed that home, so I drove out there and sure enough, there was Shane right outside the house! I wanted to shake him but that would have been a bad idea. Suddenly, sadness took over me. I almost felt like I had failed my children. I was on the brink of a breakdown but I resorted to what I knew best—pulling myself together, trying to see the light in the dark, and opting to first discipline Shane on the repercussions of running away, then I went into Mama mode but on the inside, I was struggling with many different emotions. First I really wanted to whoop him for pulling that stunt, and I knew I needed a good cry but now was not the time.

Each time I feel myself on the verge of breaking, I remind myself that there are always bigger problems than mine. I choose to smile through my sadness, to find lessons in the pain, and to carry those lessons forward as I keep dancing through life. After all, Shane was safe—that was enough to put a smile on my face. I will deal with the breakdown later.

Daily Affirmations

January 1

Change doesn't wait for fear to pass; it happens when I decide to move forward despite the fear. Courage is not the absence of fear, but the willingness to embrace it and grow through it.

January 2

Even when fear whispers, "Stay where it's safe," change calls me to step forward. Growth begins the moment I take a leap, even if my legs are shaking.

January 3

I will make mistakes, but I will not beat myself up for getting things wrong or trusting the wrong people.

January 4

I am resilient and open to learning from every experience, even the challenging ones.

January 5

I trust the process of change and allow it to shape me into my best self.

January 6

I will have realistic expectations and understand that along the way, I will fall but I am determined to be my biggest cheerleader and will pick myself up and celebrate my small wins.

January 7

I choose to focus on what I can control and let go of what I cannot.

January 8

This is my journey. Comparison is the thief of joy and will become a distraction. I am determined to stay on my own unique path.

January 9

I will embrace each day as a new opportunity to make progress and will see my setbacks as lessons.

January 10

I give myself permission to redefine my story and rewrite it as I see fit.

January 11

I am at peace with the past and focused on what I can create in the present.

January 12

I trust myself to make choices that align with my true purpose.

January 13

I will protect my inner peace. Boundaries are not selfish; they are an act of self-love, so I will create them and those who care about me will respect them.

January 14

I am worthy of success, love, and happiness. I reclaim it. I am worthy.

January 15

I release fear and allow courage to guide my next steps.

January 16

Today, I show up for myself with love, patience, and compassion.

January 17

Today, I will embrace the power of persistence. The road may be long, but every step I take builds momentum. I will not give up on myself or my dreams because my breakthrough may be close. Good results don't occur overnight.

January 18

I release fear and allow courage to guide my next steps.

January 19

Today, I will take time to rest and recharge. Productivity is important, but so is taking care of my well-being. No one can pour from an empty cup, so I will make self-care my priority.

January 20

I am grateful for the strength within me that has carried me this far.

January 21

Fear is the companion of change, but courage is what carries you through. Even when you're uncertain, trust that every step you take toward change will lead to something greater.

January 22

I will stop waiting for the perfect moment because there will never be a perfect time to start, so I'll take action today. Change doesn't wait for fear to fade. It asks me to move forward despite it because staying still is far more frightening than the unknown ahead. I will seek opportunities that move me closer to my goal.

January 23

Today, I choose to let go of limiting beliefs and see what I am truly capable of.

January 24

Today, I will let go of the need to control every outcome and accept that some things are beyond my control, and that's OK.

January 25

My past does not define my future. Whatever mistakes or setbacks I have faced are only part of my story. I choose to learn from them.

January 26

I know that fear is part of change, so I am willing to face it. I give myself permission to be vulnerable. Change may feel like stepping into the dark, but it's in those moments that I will be able to find the true light.

January 27

I have the strength to overcome any challenge even though life may throw obstacles my way. I got this.

January 28

I will not allow fear to dictate my feelings. I will push through and find courage. I will be brave.

January 29

I welcome change with an open mind and heart, ready to embrace all it brings.

January 30

I will keep showing up for myself, even when the results aren't immediate. Every small effort adds up over time, leading me closer to my goals.

January 31

As I close this month, I commit to carrying my resilience, courage, and openness forward, ready for all the new beginnings yet to come.

End-of-Month Reflections

Was I scared? Like hell I was. But I had no choice, so I stepped into my new life as a single mom, a single woman, and no longer a homeowner. It felt different, and I knew it wasn't going to be an easy journey. I put my new life into perspective like this—it was like walking into a party I never asked to attend, but now I had to be there. The music was playing, and I had to find my rhythm. I didn't have to dance to every song or talk to everyone, but I had to engage in some way. Life is about knowing when to act or react. Sometimes, the only choice we have is to face the music.

And so, as January comes to a close, remember that new beginnings are not just about grand resolutions or sweeping transformations. They are about planting seeds. Some seeds take time to sprout, but that doesn't mean they aren't growing beneath the surface. Trust the process. Believe in the power of consistent effort and remember that each day is a chance to start anew.

February

The Month of Self-Love, Acceptance, and Gratitude

February is often known as the month of love, but this time, we're focusing on the most important kind of love—self-love. Self-love isn't selfish; it's the foundation upon which all other love is built. It's about learning to accept yourself as you are, celebrating your strengths, and forgiving your flaws. This month will also be about gratitude, which goes hand-in-hand with self-love. Gratitude shifts your mindset from what's lacking to what's abundant in your life. Together, self-love and gratitude will create space for you to grow, heal, and step into your most authentic self.

Personal Reflection: The Journey to Self-Love

Learning to love myself was one of the hardest journeys I've ever embarked on. Don't get me wrong; I am a very confident woman who knows her worth and understands what I bring to the table. However, I tend to put the feelings of others ahead of mine. I was selfless and too giving. I will give even when I have nothing left inside of me. I forgot that you can't pour from an empty cup. I did this with family, friends, and in all my relationships. People will take as long as you are willing to give and since I am such a pleaser, I just kept on giving until I was empty. I looked around and there was hardly anyone left standing around to now pour into me.

After my divorce, I did get back into the dating game, and what a cruel world that is. I truly did not understand what that world was like. I had met my first husband at a young age, so hardly understood the nuance of the dating world. Imagine a girl with no real-world experience stepping into this new world after being married for twenty years. Oh, the lies and deceit but the worst was my naivete. I actually believed everything I was told and each time, I got my poor heart shattered into little pieces. Thank God it was not too many times because Lord knows that my temper would have led me in the wrong direction—Perhaps somewhere wearing my favorite color, orange, permanently – I love orange but not that much - you get my drift right? What I did learn during this process was that I do not have to wait to die and go to hell to see the face of the devil because in my single days; I met him and he came dressed in a suit. The first lesson was not to trust anyone. Well, that was hard since I wanted to treat people how I expected to get treated but apparently, that is a recipe for heartbreak and so I learned to just be selfish.

Self-love is practice, not a one-time decision. I had to relearn how to be kind to myself. I had to forgive myself for the choices I made, for the times I stayed in situations that no longer served me, and for all the times I gave others more chances than they deserved in hopes that they were truly sorry and that this time was the last time and that it would never happen again. I made it all about me and there is nothing wrong with that.

Self-love is not about ego or vanity; it's about seeing yourself as worthy, just as you are. I started doing small things, like taking time to rest without guilt, journaling my feelings, and reminding myself every day that I am deserving of love, not just from others, but from myself. If there's one thing I've learned, it's that the journey to self-love requires patience, but it's the most rewarding love story you'll ever have. I also learned to say no. What a powerful two-letter word.

Embracing Me

I am my own steady ground,
A quiet strength, a gentle sound.
In a world of chaos and demand,
I hold my heart with my own hand.

I am enough, just as I am,
A spark of light, a steady flame.
No need for more, no need for less,
In my own company, I find rest.

I see the scars, each line, and crease,
The stories told my soul's release.
These marks are mine, they speak of grace,
Of battles won, of dreams I chase.

I lift myself when no one can,
A warm embrace, my own best friend.
For love begins with looking in,
With kindness growing from within.

So here I stand, both whole and free,
A work in progress, beautifully me.
                                        —*Annise*

Daily Affirmations

February 1

I am enough, just as I am. I embrace the beauty and uniqueness in me and let go of the need to compare myself to others.

February 2

My worth isn't determined by my accomplishments. I am deserving of love and respect, and I know who I am

February 3

Today, I choose self-forgiveness and allow myself the grace to move forward because I deserve it.

February 4

I am not perfect. I release the need for perfection.

February 5

I will practice kindness not just towards others but to myself. I will replace self-criticism with words of encouragement.

February 6

I will honor my body by listening to what it needs today and avoid negative conversations and company. My body deserves to rest in a positive space.

February 7

Today I will celebrate my progress, no matter how small, and acknowledge that growth takes time. I will not beat myself up for not getting it right all the time.

February 8

I release all negative self-talk and transform my mindset into a positive place. Whenever I catch myself thinking self-critical thoughts, I will pause and reframe them with positivity. Today, I will strive to replace "I can't" with "I am capable."

February 9

I embrace all my imperfections. They are what makes you real, relatable, and human. I accept that flaws are a natural part of life and that they do not define my worth.

February 10

I deserve love and care. Today I will take a break to focus on something that brings me peace, whether it's reading, meditating, or simply being present with yourself.

February 11

I am grateful for the journey I am on, even if it is not where I imagined.

February 12

Progress is more important than perfection, so today I give myself permission to grow at my own pace.

February 13

I acknowledge my strength and how far I have come. I have survived every difficult day up until now, and that is something to be proud of. I give myself grace.

February 14

Today I vow to treat myself in an exceptionally loving way. I deserve the same love and affection I shower others with. To be able to love others, I must love myself first.

February 15

Today, I honor myself for all that I have achieved and endured. Self-gratitude is the foundation of true self-love and acceptance.

February 16

Growth is a journey, not a race. I release the need to have everything figured out. I am exactly where I need to be and trust that each day I am evolving.

February 17

I appreciate the opportunity to grow and evolve in my own time. I am not in competition with anyone – this is my race – my journey – my life.

February 18

Setting boundaries is an act of self-respect. Today, I protect my energy and well-being by learning to say no when necessary and honoring my own needs.

February 19

I release the need for outside validation. I am worthy of love and happiness as I am. My value comes from within, and I trust in my own choices.

February 20

In stillness, I find peace. Today, I will take a few moments to pause, breathe, and reconnect with myself, knowing that clarity comes in the quiet.

February 21

I am not my past. I let go of old regrets and mistakes. Each day offers a fresh beginning, and I am free to create the future I desire.

February 22

I surround myself with positivity. I choose people, activities, and environments that uplift me and protect my peace.

February 23

I am enough, exactly as I am. I let go of the need to prove myself and embrace my inherent worth, knowing I am loved and accepted just as I am.

February 24

I practice patience with myself, understanding that growth takes time. I accept setbacks as part of my journey and trust in my progress.

February 25

My uniqueness is my strength. Today, I celebrate what sets me apart, for it is the essence of my individuality.

February 26

My relationship with myself is sacred. I invest in it daily through acts of self-care, self-respect, and self-compassion, knowing that I am worth the effort.

February 27

Self-love is not selfish; it's essential. By nurturing myself, I am better equipped to support others. I fill my own cup and share the overflow freely.

February 28

As the month closes, I reflect on the love I've cultivated for myself. Self-love is a continuous journey, and I commit to nourishing myself with kindness, gratitude, and acceptance every day.

End-of-the-Month Reflection

The greatest part of my self-love journey was realizing that I was in love with myself and that I enjoyed spending time with just me. All my life, I had spent in a crowd—big family, a large circle of friends, big lunch group at work—and suddenly I decided to rediscover myself, and what a revelation that was.

Self-love is not a destination; it's a daily practice. This month, you've been reminded that self-love is about accepting who you are in all your complexity. We all have moments of doubt, times when we feel less than perfect, but those moments do not define us. Embrace your journey and your growth, and most importantly, be gentle with yourself and learn to say no.

March

Embracing Growth and Transformation

March is a time of transformation. As the seasons shift and nature awakens, it reminds us that change is not only natural but necessary for growth. Just as the world around us begins to bloom, we too can lean into this energy of renewal, shedding old layers and embracing the new. Growth is rarely comfortable, but it is always rewarding. This month is about stepping outside of your comfort zone, embracing change, and cultivating the courage to transform into the person you are becoming.

Personal Reflection: The Power of Letting Go

March has always been a time of growth and rebirth for me. It is the month where I consciously ask myself, "Am I holding on to something I should let go?" More often than not, the answer is yes. Letting go is never easy, whether it's a relationship, a job, or even an old way of thinking. But with each release comes the freedom to make room for something new.

Letting go isn't always just about emotional or mental release—it can also be a powerful, external act of transformation. For me, it was the decision to cut off all my hair and start fresh. I had held on to my hair for so long, almost as if it represented a certain identity, an image of who I thought I needed to be or how I wanted to be perceived by the world. But in truth, my hair had become symbolic of the weight I was carrying—the emotional baggage, societal expectations for what a girl should look like, and, in many ways, a version of myself that no longer felt authentic. Starting over can often feel terrifying, but it's also incredibly empowering so I decided to let go of the long mane that I had nurtured for years. I am not my hair.

The act of cutting it off wasn't just about changing my appearance; it was about liberation. It was a bold, external reflection of an internal shift—a physical manifestation of my decision to let go of old narratives, relationships, and parts of myself that were no longer serving me. There was something immensely freeing about watching those strands fall away, knowing that I was shedding more than just hair. I was releasing years of expectations, mistakes, doubts, and fears.

I clearly recall that day I walked into the beauty parlor. Tracey was the only hairdresser I could trust for this big chop. She was clearly happy to see me until she heard what my request was. "Cut off all your hair?" she asked loudly with her eyes so big I thought they would fall out. I calmly replied with a simple yes and shook my head to support my response. I was certain this was part of my new journey and new beginnings. Tracey empathically replied, "Missy, you are going to have to find you another hairdresser because I am damn sure not going to cut the hair I just helped you grow in the last three years," and a few cuss words in her DC accent. No way was I going to have another hairdresser do the honors. It was either Tracey or I was keeping my hair but I was determined. I offered her some of her favorite dark chocolates from London; I had just returned from a visit and knew she loved their chocolates. I sat in her chair and spilled my guts out. The funny thing with hairdressers, they somehow end up becoming our therapists. By the end of our talk, Tracey had her scissors and said, "Gurl, I'm doing this but I sure wanna cry. This don't feel right, boo." She did cut off all my hair, and it felt like a release. It felt absolutely right. I had no regrets.

By cutting my hair, I took control. It was my way of saying, "I choose to start anew." It wasn't about beauty standards or making a statement to others—it was deeply personal. It was about me stepping into a space where I no longer felt confined by my past or anyone else's perceptions. It was my reset button, a way to visually and tangibly mark a new chapter in my life.

And the beauty of it? Hair grows back. Just like we rebuild ourselves after letting go. Growth is inevitable, and each step is an opportunity to nurture something new, something more aligned with the person you're becoming. Letting go, whether it's internal or external, isn't an ending; it's the beginning of a transformation.

This month, I encourage you to embrace your own transformation. Trust the process, even when it's uncomfortable. Let go of what no longer serves you, and make space for the growth that is coming.

Daily Affirmations

March 1

Growth is uncomfortable, but staying the same is far more painful in the long run. Choose to lean into the discomfort, knowing that it's guiding you toward something greater.

March 2

Embrace the unknown. You don't need to have everything figured out. Trust that each step you take leads you to where you need to be.

March 3

Transformation requires letting go. Release the habits, thoughts, or relationships that no longer serve your highest good. Trust that what's meant for you will find you once you make space for it.

March 4

Don't rush the process. Just like a seed planted in the ground, your growth takes time. Be patient with yourself, and trust that change is happening, even if you can't see it yet.

March 5

Remember that growth isn't linear. There will be setbacks, but every step forward, no matter how small, is progress. Celebrate the small victories along the way.

March 6

Honor the changes you've already made. Reflect on where you were a year ago, five years ago, and see how far you've come. You are stronger, wiser, and more capable than you give yourself credit for.

March 7

You don't have to do it all at once. Focus on one area of your life where you want to see growth and give it your attention. Small, consistent actions lead to big changes over time.

March 8

Transformation starts with your mindset. Shift your focus from obstacles to opportunities. The way you think about your challenges will determine how you approach them.

March 9

Release the fear of failure. Failure is not the opposite of success; it's part of the process. Each mistake you make brings you one step closer to your goals.

March 10

Your journey is yours alone. Stop comparing your progress to others. Everyone's path looks different, and that's what makes each story unique. Focus on your growth, not theirs.

March 11

Be open to change, even when it's unexpected. Life has a way of shifting plans, but sometimes those detours lead to the most beautiful destinations.

March 12

Take a leap of faith. If you're waiting for the right time, you'll be waiting forever. The only way to grow is to take the first step, even if you're unsure of the outcome.

March 13

Trust in your resilience. You have overcome challenges before, and you will again. Remember that you've survived 100 percent of your hardest days. You are stronger than you know.

March 14

Growth often comes disguised as a challenge. Don't be discouraged when things get difficult. Every obstacle is an opportunity to learn and grow.

March 15

Embrace your evolution. You don't have to be the same person you were yesterday, last month, or last year. Allow yourself the freedom to grow, change, and evolve.

March 16

Growth requires resilience. Challenges may arise, but you have the strength to overcome them. Remember, it's the difficult moments that shape you into a stronger, wiser version of yourself.

March 17

Be mindful of your energy. Protect your peace by surrounding yourself with positivity and letting go of toxic influences. When you create a positive environment, your growth will flourish.

March 18

Surround yourself with people who support your growth. The company you keep has a profound impact on your journey. Choose to spend time with those who uplift, encourage, and inspire you.

March 19

Remember that setbacks are part of the process. Don't let one bad day convince you that you're not making progress. Every journey has its ups and downs.

March 20

Give yourself permission to rest. Growth requires energy, and it's OK to take a break when you need it. Rest is a vital part of the transformation process.

March 21

Today is the perfect day to start something new. Whether it's a habit, a project, or a mindset, use today to take the first step toward something you've been wanting to change.

March 22

Growth happens outside of your comfort zone. If you're feeling uncomfortable, that's a sign that you're on the right track. Lean into discomfort, knowing that it's leading to something better.

March 23

You are capable of more than you think. Don't limit yourself to doubts or fears. Believe in your potential and take action toward your goals.

March 24

Transformation is not about becoming someone new; it's about uncovering the person you've always been. Trust in your journey and allow yourself to grow into the fullest version of yourself.

March 25

The hardest part of growth is often letting go of what's familiar. But remember, you cannot make space for new opportunities if you're still holding onto the past.

March 26

Be gentle with yourself during this time of transformation. Growth takes time, and it's OK if you don't have all the answers yet. Trust in the process and know that you're exactly where you need to be.

March 27

Celebrate your resilience. Think of a time when you faced a challenge and came out stronger. Let that be a reminder of your strength as you continue to grow.

March 28

Growth requires you to be vulnerable. Don't be afraid to ask for help when you need it. You don't have to do it all alone, and there is strength in leaning on others.

March 29

Be intentional with your energy. Focus on what matters most to you and let go of the distractions that pull you away from your growth. You have the power to choose where you invest your time and energy.

March 30

You are constantly evolving. Embrace the changes happening within you, and trust that each step is bringing you closer to your fullest potential.

March 31

As this month of transformation comes to an end, reflect on how far you've come. Celebrate the growth you've experienced and look forward to the new beginnings that lie ahead.

End-of-Month Reflection

As March comes to a close, take a moment to reflect on the journey of growth and transformation you've embraced this month. This time of renewal has invited you to release what no longer fits into your desired life style, opening space for new possibilities and growth. Much like nature's cycle, transformation isn't a single act but a series of intentional choices, each shedding a layer of what was, making room for what is to come.

Growth is rarely easy, but it is always meaningful. Trust that each step you've taken, no matter how small or seemingly insignificant, has moved you closer to becoming your truest self and unlocking your fullest potential. Every bit of progress is worth celebrating because it means you're evolving. Celebrate the courage it took to let go, whether of old habits, fears, or expectations.

Acknowledge the discomfort that often accompanies change for it is in those uneasy moments that true growth takes place. As you move forward, carry the lessons you've learned and the strength you've gained. Know that each step you take is guiding you toward a more authentic, aligned version of yourself.

Embrace the beauty of this new season with gratitude and optimism and remember that transformation is an ongoing journey. As you enter the next chapter, keep nurturing your growth, trust in the path you're creating, and welcome the abundant possibilities that lie ahead.

April

The Power of Forgiveness, Moving Forward, and Unplugging

I have learned that letting go of the pain others have caused is peaceful but I also know that I need to forgive myself for mistakes I have made and held onto. Forgiveness is freeing, and while it's often difficult, I've learned that it's necessary for my growth. I once believed that forgiveness meant excusing the behavior of those who hurt me, but I've come to understand that it's more about freeing myself from the grip of resentment.

In a world that rarely slows down, I realized that moving forward sometimes requires unplugging or blocking not just from digital distractions but also from the overthinking and emotional clutter that can cloud our judgment. I've learned to value moments of silence, giving my mind space to rest, my heart the chance to heal, and my spirit the opportunity to reset.

Unplugging allows me to focus on my own well-being, reassess my priorities, and move forward without carrying the burdens of the past. It's not about erasing memories or forgetting people; it's about actively choosing peace over pain, and growth over stagnation.

This month, I encourage you to release any need for validation or closure from others. Instead, offer yourself the forgiveness and peace you truly deserve. As you unplug from distractions or distance yourself from those who have let you down, you'll find the clarity to move forward with freedom and purpose.

Personal Reflection: Love Remains but Access Denied!

There comes a time in life when we are faced with the difficult decision to let go of people we've cared for, even when we still love them. This has been one of my hardest lessons—learning that loving someone doesn't always mean keeping them in your life. Sometimes, no matter how much love we have for a person, we have to create space for our own well-being and growth.

I think we all at some point in our lives have had to let go of someone we love because "love was just not enough" anymore. I have had to make that painful decision a few times and it is always tough. But sometimes, we have to release some folks from our lives because no matter how many chances they get, they never change. We must accept that the relationships we once shared with some will never be the same because so many boundaries have been crossed and trust broken and the only path to peace is to walk away.

It is never an easy choice especially when there is history and so many memories. You will have moments when guilt will take over and self-doubt as to whether you are making the right choice. For me, as I get older, peace and respect are more important than tenure so that is my yardstick and once I begin to feel that they are in jeopardy or being questioned, then it's time to make a decision. As my daughter, Shania, once wisely told me, "Give people the same energy they give you." I've had to learn the hard way, but I understand now that my time and energy are precious and that respect is paramount. If you were to ask my family or closest friends who would make the first call to make peace after a disagreement, the unanimous answer would likely be me.

For a long time, I took pride in this, seeing myself as the peacemaker, the one who always reached out first. But as I've matured emotionally, I've come to see how this habit gave others permission to mistreat me without consequence. I can no longer rely on hope that if given just one more chance, they will not repeat the unacceptable behavior so I am brave enough these days to know when to cut the cord. Letting go doesn't mean I stopped loving them; it simply means I put my emotional well-being first.

Whilst this process of letting go has been challenging it has also been liberating. I recognize that self-love sometimes means making difficult decisions for our own well-being, even if it hurts. And I've learned that not everyone who comes into our lives is meant to stay forever. Some people are only there to teach us lessons—lessons about ourselves, about boundaries, and about the power of letting go.

As I look back on some of my decision lately to end some relationships, I hold no grudge...ok...I try not to hold any grudge but rather remain focused on the happier times. I've learned that sometimes love is not about holding on, but about knowing when to let go. I've made peace with the fact that some people do not deserve front row seat to my life movie or behind the scenes special pass. I will forever cherish all the good times and the memories we created together but the curtain's drawn - Love remains, but ACCESS DENIED.

Daily Affirmations

April 1

Forgiveness is a gift I give myself. It allows me to release the weight of the past and make space for new possibilities.

April 2

Resentment only holds me back. I choose to let go and embrace the peace that forgiveness brings.

April 3

I forgive myself for my past mistakes. I am human, and each experience has made me wiser and stronger.

April 4

Today, I move forward with intention, leaving the past behind and focusing on what lies ahead.

April 5

I unplug from the noise and distractions that drain my energy, reconnecting with my inner peace.

April 6

Forgiveness doesn't excuse the behavior, but it releases me from the control that pain has over my life.

April 7

I release the need to be right. Peace and reconciliation matter more than winning an argument.

April 8

Today, I unplug from negativity, choosing to protect my energy and surround myself with positivity.

April 9

Forgiveness is an act of strength, not weakness. I trust in my ability to heal and move forward.

April 10

With an open heart, I let go of past pain and welcome new opportunities for growth and joy.

April 11

I unplug from distractions and focus on the things that bring me joy and fulfillment.

April 12

I forgive myself for the expectations I didn't meet. I accept that I'm doing my best and that is enough.

April 13

Moving forward requires patience. Healing takes time, and I trust the process of my growth.

April 14

I choose peace over anger. I release the pain of the past and embrace the healing power of forgiveness.

April 15

I let go of the past and focus on the present. The future is full of possibilities waiting for me.

April 16

I release self-judgment and regret, forgiving myself and stepping into a future of self-acceptance.

April 17

I move forward with gratitude, appreciating the lessons I've learned and the person I've become.

April 18

Today, I unplug from the chaos and give myself the gift of stillness and rest. In the stillness, I find clarity.

April 19

I forgive others without expecting an apology. I create my own closure and choose to heal on my terms.

April 20

I move forward with courage, trusting that I have the strength to face whatever lies ahead.

April 21

I unplug from overthinking, giving my mind space to relax and allowing life to unfold naturally.

April 22

I forgive myself for missed opportunities, knowing that new chances are always on the horizon.

April 23

I move forward with purpose, aligning my actions with my intentions to create a life that reflects my values.

April 24

I am special – I am enough! I unplug from comparison and trust that my unique path is leading me where I need to go.

April 25

Forgiveness brings freedom. I release the emotional chains that keep me stuck in the past.

April 26

I move forward without fear, trusting that each step will bring greater clarity and strength.

April 27

I unplug from my to-do list and give myself permission to rest without guilt. Rest is part of the process.

April 28

I forgive those who hurt me, not because they deserve it, but because I deserve peace.

April 29

I move forward with forgiveness in my heart, releasing resentment and making space for love and joy.

April 30

As this month ends, I reflect on the forgiveness I've extended and the progress I've made. I carry this peace with me as I continue to grow.

End-of-Month Reflection

Forgiveness is not always easy, but it is always freeing. As April comes to a close, take a moment to acknowledge the healing you've embraced this month. Each act of forgiveness, whether toward yourself or others, has allowed you to release the weight of the past and move forward with a lighter heart. The peace you've found through this process will continue to guide you as you grow. Remember, moving forward is not just about letting go; it's about stepping into a future full of possibilities without the burden of yesterday holding you back. Forgiveness is really for you—not for those who have hurt you—so do not allow them to hold you back because you are still holding onto old grudges or pain.

May
The Month of Reflection and Accountability

May is a time to pause, look inward, and take stock of where you are in your life. Reflection allows you to better understand your journey, your decisions, and the growth you've experienced. Alongside reflection comes accountability, the practice of owning your actions, choices, and their outcomes.

It is a good practice and part of one's self-care to have the discipline to take a look at yourself and say, "Where could I have done better?" or "What have I been avoiding?" Without self-reflection, there's no way to truly grow. Reflection is about understanding not just what has happened, but how I have contributed to my circumstances, both the good and the bad.

Accountability has been another powerful lesson. It's easy to blame external factors—other people, situations beyond my control—but growth requires owning my part in every experience. I've learned that accountability isn't about assigning blame; it's about reclaiming my power. When I take responsibility for my life, I give myself the freedom to make changes, learn from past mistakes, and move forward with purpose.

There have been times when I've made excuses, avoiding the hard truths in favor of comfort or denial. But accountability asks more from us. It's about consistency, self-discipline, and recommitting to the promises I've made to myself.

This month, I commit to reflecting on where I am, accepting the reality of what is, and holding myself accountable for the steps I need to take next.

In moments where I falter, I remind myself that reflection is not about perfection; it's about progress. Accountability is not a burden; it's the key to unlocking a future where I am fully in control of my choices and growth.

Boy have I taken some wrong turns in this life! But we are allowed to fail. The real problem is not learning from our mistakes or not taking responsibility for the role we played in some of the outcomes of our life choices.

I have trusted the wrong person, picked the wrong partner, not prepared enough for an exam or an interview, made the wrong fashion choice, and sometimes said the wrong things, but the key is I know always try to go back and replay it all so that I can learn from that fall or fail. I am not perfect in any stance.

The Power of an Apology

I've never had a problem admitting when I'm wrong. I don't allow pride or fear of vulnerability to get in the way of being accountable for my actions - it's simply about owning the situation and doing what's right. I am not perfect – I make mistakes, I hurt others, albeit unintentionally but still and whenever I do or find myself in a problematic situation, I really try my best to look at the problem honestly and see what role I played in it. Acknowledging my mistakes or shortcomings isn't something I shy away from—if anything, I see it as a chance to grow and do better.

There's a moment I'll always remember that reaffirmed this mindset. It was during a disagreement with my daughter. We both said things in the heat of the moment, and the tension hung in the air long after the conversation ended. As soon as I took a step back and reflected, I realized I had touched a nerve. I didn't need to make excuses or justify myself—I just needed to own it. The next day, I sat down with her and said, "I'm sorry. I shouldn't have spoken to you like that." We should normalize apologizing to our children too.

Apologizing to my daughter in that moment showed her that I respected her. It was also a teachable moment for her to realize that it is ok to be accountable and to talk about it. The atmosphere lightened, and we were able to talk openly about the situation. I think it was important for her to see that apologizing isn't a sign of weakness, but rather an opportunity to strengthen relationships.

Being able to say "I'm sorry" has always come naturally to me because I've never seen it as a weakness although others have perceived it as that. Admitting when we are wrong isn't about diminishing oneself; it's about growing, being accountable, and creating space for healing. Life doesn't always go as planned, and mistakes happen. But in those moments, we should not be afraid to take a step back and recognize our part in the issue. The ability to reflect on our actions, without letting pride get in the way, is a character strength.

In the end, I believe that saying "I'm sorry" is a powerful tool for growth, not just in relationships with others but in our relationship with ourselves. It's a way to acknowledge where we can improve and a chance to make things right. As I've navigated through life's ups and downs, I've come to see that owning up to our mistakes is a testament to our character—and it's something that should never be feared. And sometimes, we even need to apologize to ourselves. Yes, that too.

PERSONAL REFLECTION

Perfectly Imperfect

I've trusted wrong hands, and picked wrong hearts,
Stumbled through paths that tore me apart.
I've faced exams I wasn't ready to meet,
Showed up ill-prepared with no time to retreat.

I've said the wrong words when silence was due,
Made mistakes that I wish I could undo.
But in every misstep, in every fall,
I replay the moments and learn through it all.

I'm not perfect, I never claim to be,
But I lean on reflection and take accountability.
For every failure, for every regret,
Is a lesson I carry, not one to forget.

I stumble and fall, but I rise once more,
With each misstep, I learn to restore.
Imperfect, I stand, yet stronger each day,
Guided by lessons as I find my way.

—*Annise*

Daily Affirmations

May 1

Reflection is a tool for self-growth. I take time today to look inward and assess my personal journey with honesty and compassion.

May 2

Accountability begins with truth. I own my actions, my choices, and the role I play in shaping my life.

May 3

True accountability requires confronting the areas in my life where I can improve. I face these with courage, knowing growth is on the other side.

May 4

Reflection isn't just about mistakes. I celebrate my progress, no matter how small, because every step forward matters.

May 5

I hold myself accountable for the habits that hold me back and commit to creating ones that align with my goals.

May 6

Reflection reveals patterns. I notice the recurring behaviors and thoughts in my life and choose which ones to nurture and which to release.

May 7

Being accountable means accepting my role in every situation. I take ownership of my actions and stop looking for others to blame.

May 8

I reflect on my core values today and ensure my actions are aligned with what truly matters to me.

May 9

I am responsible for how I respond to life's challenges. Today, I hold myself accountable for how I manage my emotions.

May 10

Reflection on my past choices gives me clarity. I learn from my experiences without regret and apply those lessons moving forward.

May 11

I commit to taking small, consistent actions toward my goals. Accountability is not about perfection, but about progress.

May 12

I reflect on my relationships and hold myself accountable for the energy I bring into them. I nurture the connections that matter most.

May 13

Accountability requires consistency. Today, I recommit to showing up for myself and my goals, even when it's difficult.

May 14

Reflection brings clarity to what truly matters. I focus on what aligns with my values and let go of what no longer serves me.

May 15

I hold myself accountable for how I spend my time. I use this precious resource wisely, directing it toward my personal growth.

May 16

Self-reflection requires patience. I am kind to myself as I look back on my journey, knowing that growth is a process.

May 17

Quit making excuses and start taking action. Ask yourself what small steps you can take today toward your goals.

May 18

Reflection often brings discomfort, but it is necessary for growth. I give myself space to deeply assess where I can improve.

May 19

Accountability includes honoring my personal boundaries. I protect my energy by setting and enforcing limits that support my well-being.

May 20

I reflect on my progress this year and adjust my goals as needed. I trust that growth is happening in its own time.

May 21

I am open to feedback and recognize that others can offer valuable perspectives. I listen without defensiveness and use constructive advice to grow.

May 22

I am responsible for my mindset. I hold myself accountable for creating a positive mental environment that supports my dreams.

May 23

I celebrate how far I've come. I reflect on the small victories and milestones that have shaped my journey.

May 24

I stop blaming others for my circumstances. I reclaim control by holding myself accountable for my choices and actions.

May 25

I reflect on my emotional well-being and hold myself accountable for creating balance and seeking support when needed.

May 26

Accountability includes forgiving myself for past mistakes. I release the burden of guilt and focus on learning from the past.

May 27

I take responsibility for my self-talk. I speak to myself with kindness and affirm my ability to create positive changes in my life.

May 28

I reflect on my achievements. Today, I take pride in how far I've come and the growth I've experienced.

May 29

I follow through on my commitments, both to myself and to others. Integrity is key to living a life of accountability.

May 30

Reflection creates clarity. I meditate on the lessons I've learned this month and commit to applying them in the future.

May 31

As May ends, I reflect on how accountability has shaped my growth. I carry these lessons forward as I continue to strive for integrity and self-discipline in all areas of my life.

End-of-Month Reflection

Reflection and accountability are the foundations of growth. As May comes to a close, take a moment to acknowledge the insights you've gained this month. Each time you held yourself accountable, you empowered yourself to create positive change. Remember that growth isn't about being perfect; it's about being honest with yourself, owning your actions, and making adjustments where necessary. Moving forward, continue to hold yourself accountable with kindness and integrity, knowing that true progress comes from self-awareness and the commitment to becoming your best self.

June

Developing Patience, Strength, and Balance

June is a month of gentle reflection, focusing on developing patience, inner strength, and balance. No matter where we find ourselves in life, we all share a common thread—the cycles of joy and sorrow, loss and gain, light and dark. These rhythms of life can be difficult to navigate, but the true challenge lies in learning how to remain grounded, positive, and balanced within us, no matter what the circumstances.

Life's trials often test our resilience, pushing us to the edges of our comfort zones. Yet through patience and mindfulness, we can return to a place of calm and centeredness. This month, the focus is on nurturing both mind and spirit, embracing challenges as opportunities to grow stronger, and finding equilibrium in every area of life. By practicing patience, building strength, and seeking balance, you create a foundation of peace and resilience that will carry you through the storms ahead. During this month, I wanted to focus on how we use patience and strength to help find a balance both in our career world and personal lives. I am especially reminded of how important it was for me to blend these two in my leadership roles, especially in a volunteer capacity.

Personal Reflection: Balancing Act of Leadership

Leading in a volunteer space can be one of the most rewarding yet challenging experiences. It requires an immense amount of patience, especially when you're giving so much of yourself without expecting much in return. In these selfless roles, moments of disillusionment can arise when your efforts go unappreciated or when backbiting and disagreement rear their heads. Yet despite these difficulties, true fulfillment lies not in recognition, but in knowing that your efforts contribute to something greater than yourself.

My journey into volunteer leadership began unexpectedly about twenty years ago. One of our cousins invited my sister Jemi and me to a fundraiser for our alma mater. We went, eager to support the cause and reunite with old friends. While the event didn't have the fanfare I had imagined, it did rekindle connections. And that night, by some stroke of serendipity, I found myself asked to cohost the event. Perhaps it was the way my handmade dress, courtesy of Jemi, shimmered under the lights, or maybe they saw something in me I hadn't yet recognized. Nervously, I accepted the microphone, and from that moment, something clicked. "Wow, I can do this all night," I thought to myself. I knew I was killing it by the looks of approval on the faces of all the other guests and the way Jemi kept smiling at me so proudly. I realized I had a natural gift for public speaking, and that night, a passion was ignited.

Fast forward to today, I am still in the organization and proud to say I am a two-term president who has had quite a successful administration though not without some sweat, blood, and tears. Navigating leadership, particularly among women, can sometimes come with its share of challenges. The occasional misunderstandings and differing opinions are natural human experiences. These trials, while difficult, offer opportunities for growth and reflection. In these moments, developing patience becomes crucial. It's about understanding that not everyone will see the vision the same way, and that's ok. Leadership is about keeping your focus on the cause, learning from every interaction, and building resilience through it all.

Maturity also plays a big role in some of these minor disagreements. When I look back at myself a decade ago, I can see how much I've grown. I would have handled poorly many of the challenges I face now if they happened in my younger years, so this allows me to give grace to others because I know that I was there before. Today, I understand that some of the aggression we face from others are not necessarily personal attacks even though it may appear so. I've also had to accept that some individuals are determined to see only the negative, to stir up discord rather than contribute constructively.

In the beginning, I made the mistake of trying to win these people over, thinking that if I included them more, they would see my good intentions. That is after all my personality. Remember, I can be naive, and sometimes the old me creeps back in. When that happens, I have to check myself and remind myself not to keep making the same mistakes or expecting people to change—or for everyone to approve of me. That, too, is one of the mistakes failed leaders make. A leader who strives to be loved by all will fail because they will keep changing their strategies and moving the goalpost to please everyone. A true leader must be willing to take the beating. You get to wear the crown and take full credit when all is fine so also be prepared to take the fall when things don't work out or goals are not met.

One must always be cognizant of the fact that in any capacity where there is a group of people, there will always be some, even if only a handful, who thrive on creating chaos, and no amount of kindness or inclusivity would change their behavior. They are determined to rock the boat even if the water is calm. The best action in such a situation is to continue to take the right steps; play by the rules; be inclusive and fair; and never ever allow others to disrespect you or water down your value or your contribution. Translation—follow the rules but know your worth. Everyone is not going to like you or be your friend, especially when you are in a leadership role but as long as you lead in an unbiased way, your conscience will be clear so when your time is up and you are no longer in that space you will leave behind a record and reputation you will be proud of.

I am now in the last lap of my tenure, and I am already beginning to look back with pride at what we have accomplished. I have learned so much and met some incredible and passionate women on this journey. I am ever so grateful for the connections I have made, both internally and externally, the sisterhood we have built, and the work we have done together as a team. I have also gained some new knowledge and definitely grew as a leader and as a team player.

The key to effective leadership isn't just about being strong; it's about balancing strength with kindness, resilience with grace, and patience with persistence. There have been moments when I've had to navigate a tightrope of emotions—laughing, crying, encouraging others—and all while managing my own personal struggles. But through it all, I've learned that balance is essential.

It is important for anyone in a leadership role to understand that while "leadership" demands giving, you must also take care of yourself. Burnout is real, especially when leading in a space where recognition is minimal, and the demands are constant. The weight of responsibility can feel overwhelming, particularly when the effort and impact are often unseen. To be an effective leader, you need to replenish your energy regularly. You can't pour from an empty cup. Finding the balance between service to others and self-care is critical to long-term success.

As we move through June, remember that leadership isn't measured by applause or external validation, but by the quiet progress you make along the way. It's the lives you touch, the changes you help facilitate, and the strength you build in both yourself and others. Celebrate the small wins, honor the patience you've developed, and give yourself grace when things don't go perfectly. Stop waiting for others to thank you…allow yourself to get to a place where you are able to be so in touch with yourself, that you are fully aware of your mistakes and your achievements – that is self-empowering and humbling at the same time. Today, don't just smile at your accomplishments. Go buy yourself those flowers, heck, even start your own garden – grow them or buy them but by all means get them. You've earned them!

Daily Affirmations

June 1

Patience takes practice. Not everything unfolds on your schedule. Trust that the right things will happen in their own time, and practice grace in moments of frustration.

June 2

Strength comes not only from endurance but from knowing when to pause. Balance productivity with rest, for true strength comes from honoring the need to recharge.

June 3

I have the strength to navigate any challenge with grace and resilience, recognizing that every experience strengthens my leadership.

June 4

I cultivate patience with myself and others, understanding that growth is a gradual process.

June 5

Strength is built in moments of challenge. When you face adversity, remind yourself that every obstacle is an opportunity to grow stronger. Don't shy away from challenges. Embrace them as part of your journey.

June 6

Mindfulness is essential for balance. Take a moment today to assess where you're giving too much or too little. Adjust your focus to bring harmony into your routine and let go of what no longer serves you.

June 7

Patience is an act of self-compassion. Be gentle with yourself as you navigate life's ups and downs. Offer yourself the same kindness you extend to others.

June 8

Today, I balance assertiveness with empathy. I lead with confidence while remaining open to others' perspectives.

June 9

I welcome adversity, knowing it strengthens my resilience and leadership.

June 10

Patience is a form of wisdom. It allows you to step back, see the bigger picture, and respond thoughtfully. Let patience guide your reactions today.

June 11

Strength is quiet, not loud. True strength is found in resilience, persistence, and the ability to stay grounded even in the face of chaos. Cultivate your inner strength by staying calm, centered, and focused even in the face of adversity.

June 12

Balance requires boundaries. Protect your peace by saying no when necessary and create space for self-care. Rest is essential to maintain balance in all areas of life.

June 13

I embrace the power of patience, understanding that true progress is built with steady, intentional steps.

June 14

Today, I create balance by listening more deeply, allowing others the space to share and grow.

June 15

As a leader, I balance strength with humility, acknowledging that my team's success is our shared achievement.

June 16

Patience is essential in relationships. Allow others the space to grow, and practice understanding when things don't go as expected.

June 17

True strength is shown in how you rise after a fall. Every setback teaches you resilience. Embrace failure as a stepping stone toward growth.

June 18

Balance your aspirations with reality. While it's important to aim high, it's equally important to appreciate where you are today. Strive for growth while remaining grounded in the present.

June 19

I am resilient. My strength comes from navigating challenges with clarity, patience, and unwavering purpose.

June 20

Balance is my compass. I strive to create a harmonious environment where every team member feels valued and inspired.

June 21

Balance requires constant adjustment. Life is ever-changing, and your approach to finding balance must adapt. Stay flexible and aligned with your priorities.

June 22

I am resilient. My strength comes from navigating challenges with clarity, patience, and unwavering purpose.

June 23

Stay calm in the face of pressure, choosing to lead from a place of grounded strength and patience.

June 24

Balance isn't about giving equal time to everything; it's about aligning your energy with what truly matters. Focus on what brings you fulfillment and let go of the rest.

June 25

In moments of frustration, pause and breathe. Over time, your ability to stay calm and patient will grow, helping you handle life's challenges with more grace.

June 26

I honor my inner strength, finding the balance between pushing forward and knowing when to rest.

June 27

Balance is about harmony, not perfection. Strive for a life that feels aligned and peaceful, even if it's not perfectly balanced.

June 28

Trust in the timing of your life. Success comes at its own pace, and what looks like a delay might be part of a bigger plan unfolding perfectly for you.

June 29

Reflection is the key to growth. Take time to look back on your journey, recognize your resilience, and identify areas where you can continue to grow.

June 30

As this month comes to an end, reflect on how far you've come in developing patience, strength, and balance. Celebrate your progress and carry these qualities with you into the next phase of your journey.

End-of-Month Reflection

As June draws to a close, I find myself reflecting on the ways patience, strength, and balance have shaped my journey through the month and have allowed me to become a leader who is confident enough to delegate with trust. Leading others is rarely simple; it's a balancing act that requires resilience, understanding, and sometimes a quiet strength that holds steady even in moments of tension.

Throughout this month, I've been reminded that patience is not just about waiting but about maintaining composure and compassion through uncertainty. Patience has allowed me to truly listen, not just to words but to intentions, and to respond thoughtfully instead of reacting impulsively. That took a lot of training, time, and maturity. This understanding has enriched my relationships, created space for others to grow, and in many ways, fostered a deeper sense of trust with those I work directly with.

I know I am still a work in progress, and I continue to learn and grow every day. While I have made strides in becoming a more patient and trusting leader, there are still moments where I need to pause, reflect, and remind myself that growth is ongoing, and perfection is not the goal.

Strength has taken on new meaning as well. This month, I've come to realize that true strength is not in pushing harder but in knowing when to let go, when to rest, and when to support others rather than carrying everything alone. Strength in leadership has meant remaining grounded and confident, even when challenges arise, and being vulnerable enough to ask for help when needed.

Delegation has also been an essential lesson. As a leader, it's easy to feel as though you need to shoulder every responsibility, but delegation has taught me the value of trust and empowerment. By assigning tasks thoughtfully and allowing others to step into their strengths, I've been able to cultivate a more collaborative and capable team. Delegation has become a tool for nurturing talent and fostering growth in others, rather than a sign of stepping back. It's allowed me to focus on strategic direction, knowing that each person has a meaningful role in our collective success. Being able to trust others and delegate has also allowed me the time and space to rest confident that the task will be completed by reliable team members and that comes with trust.

Balance has been my guiding light, reminding me that to be a present leader, I must also be present for myself. It's easy to pour all our energy into our work, into others, and into our responsibilities, but I've learned that balance requires boundaries and self care. Balance has encouraged me to honor my needs without guilt, knowing that only when I'm whole can I truly give my best.

As I close this month, I am grateful for these lessons in patience, strength, and balance. They have not only shaped my leadership but also deepened my connection with myself. I am carrying these values forward, embracing the peace they bring, and striving to lead with purpose and presence in the months to come. True growth happens not in grand gestures, but in the quiet moments where you choose to persevere, find balance, and trust the process.

Pause. Reset. Reboot.

In the Pause, I Find My Breath

Life rushes forward, a steady race,
But sometimes, I need to find my space.
A moment to pause, a quiet recess,
To release the weight, to unburden stress.

In the stillness, the noise fades away,
And I hear the whispers of a brand-new day.
A gentle reboot, a reset in time,
Where clarity reigns and peace is mine.

The world can wait, just for a while,
As I reclaim my heart, my spirit, my smile.
In the pause, I find my breath again,
Renewed in strength, unbound by strain.

For life's greatest power lies in the slow,
In the moments of rest where true growth can show.
And when I return, refreshed and whole,
I move with purpose, I move with soul.

—*Annise*

July

The Month of Motivation, Hope, and Fearlessness

Now that we have paused, reset, and rebooted, let us get motivated, hopeful, and fearless!

July is the month to reignite your inner fire, channeling motivation and determination to pursue your goals with renewed energy. It's a time to look forward with optimism, trusting that better days are always ahead. Fearlessness, however, doesn't mean a lack of fear. It means courageously choosing to act despite the fears that may stand in our way.

Fear often lingers in our minds, whispering doubts that hold us back from realizing our potential. It's the voice that limits us, pushing us to make excuses and put off our dreams. This month is about breaking through that barrier. It's about letting motivation be your fuel, hopes your compass, and fearlessness your driving force as you boldly embrace each challenge and pursue your dreams.

Personal Reflection: Overcoming Fear—The Courage to Try

How much more vibrant life would be if we weren't so afraid to step beyond our comfort zones? Think of the times you've held back, crafting excuses like, "I can't," "They won't understand," or "I don't know how." Behind every excuse is the same dreaded four-letter word—fear. The fear of failure, rejection, or not being accepted is enough to keep us on the sidelines, even when we're yearning to dive in.

Fear quietly smothers our dreams, limits our potential, and stifles our relationships. Whether it's the fear of falling short or the fear of being rejected, fear isolates us and keeps us from taking bold leaps. We sometimes imagine that others have a flawless welcome waiting for them in every room or that acceptance will be effortless, but we need to remember that those expectations are often fantasies of fear.

The truth is that many of us have found ourselves trapped in this cycle. The moment we consider a new challenge or opportunity, our minds start racing toward the possible outcomes. Fear starts creeping in, crafting a web of what-ifs that keep us bound to our comfort zones. Of course, some fears are grounded in logic, protecting us from reckless risks, but many fears stem from our hesitation to step into the unknown.

What if, instead of holding back, we could break free from the grip of fear? What if we allowed ourselves to truly live and try? This month, I invite you to explore what lies beyond those boundaries. Make a list of things you've always wanted to do, those hidden desires that fear has kept you from. You don't even have to do them perfectly, and you might only do them once. But the joy and freedom you'll feel will be unforgettable. Whether it's learning to ride a bike, skydiving, standing up to speak in front of others, or finally telling someone you love them—each act will chip away at the power fear holds over you.

And since we're talking about pushing limits, let me share a personal story. For most of my adult life, I struggled with aquaphobia, a direct result of the trauma of losing my brother Henneh to drowning when he was just 27 years old. I loved the ambiance of the ocean and enjoyed being around the beach, but the thought of getting near the water triggered severe anxiety. When I became a mom, all three of my children loved to swim, and that made summer beach vacations incredibly stressful for me. I could never relax when the kids were swimming.

But that wasn't even the worst of it. Shane decided to join the swim team, and each time he competed, I must have died a thousand times. I literally became a madwoman running around the pool whenever Shane was in the water for team meets. I lost all pride, standards, class, or decorum. I can still picture myself doing that and screaming Shane's name each time he dived in because I thought he was never coming back up. I'm pretty sure the other parents were irritated by my frantic behavior, judging by the glances I received. I eventually had to explain myself to them, but still… Shane got bold enough and told me it was a bit embarrassing and kindly suggested that I stay outside whenever it was time for him to compete. But that would have made me even more anxious. What if he was drowning and no one noticed? Nope! I attended every swim meet and lost my mind each time he got into that pool.

After a while, my erratic behavior earned me the label of "Helicopter Mom." I couldn't help it—I was just terrified that my son would drown. I guess that's what trauma does to you—fear creeps in, no matter how hard you try to control it. Eventually, I realized that my fear of water was crippling me, so I decided to face it head-on and signed up for swimming lessons. Those 12 weeks were full of stress and anxiety, but I showed up. And boy, I made sure that for each class, I had on a new bathing suit—at least I could get something right. I found encouragement in others like me, and we formed a little support crew. Together, we motivated each other, going through those 12 weeks like our lives depended on it. Our kids were watching for Christ's sakes!

It got better—I got better. The first time I swam across the entire pool, I felt like I had conquered a major challenge. It was a huge achievement. My kids were proud of me, though they couldn't resist making fun of the way I flailed my arms when I swam. I didn't care—I was just ecstatic that I had faced one of my biggest fears and could check it off my list.

After the 12 weeks, it was graduation day. The instructor had the nerve to suggest that in order to receive our certificates, we each had to dive into the pool from eight feet above. For me, that was a step too far. I had made significant progress, and that was enough. No way was I going to take that dive. Personally, I felt I had already succeeded, so I told them to keep the certificate—I had nothing else to prove. "Bye, pool!" But my kids called me a wimp, and I said, "No amount of teasing or dares will make me." That was it for me. I could swim—I didn't need to dive from the platform.

In facing that fear, I learned something vital. Sometimes, overcoming fear isn't about conquering it completely or achieving perfection. It's about showing up, taking a leap, and knowing that you've chipped away at its hold. So, try something new this month. Embrace the awkwardness and don't worry about getting it right. Let motivation, hope, and courage define your journey, and celebrate each step forward, no matter how small.

Daily Affirmations

July 1

Motivation fuels my progress. I set my intentions for this month, knowing that each step forward brings me closer to my goals.

July 2

Release the fear of failure and replace it with the excitement of new possibilities. Every attempt is a step closer to success.

July 3

Today, take one bold step toward your goals, trusting that courage grows with every step you take.

July 4

Stay motivated by focusing on your why. Why did you start this journey? What drives you to keep going? Remind yourself of your purpose and let that inspire you to push through challenges.

July 5

My fears are temporary, but my courage is everlasting. I focus on what I can achieve, not on what might go wrong.

July 6

I choose to see fear as an opportunity for growth. Each time I face my fears, I grow stronger, braver, and more resilient.

July 7

Motivation is built through small, consistent actions. Don't wait for a burst of inspiration. Start today with one small task that brings you closer to your goal, and let the momentum build from there.

July 8

Hope is about believing in possibilities, even when the odds seem against you. Stay hopeful today by focusing on solutions, not problems. Trust that every challenge has a way through it.

July 9

Fearlessness grows from self-belief. Trust in your abilities and remind yourself of your past successes. If you've conquered challenges before, you can conquer them again.

July 10

Stay motivated by celebrating progress, no matter how small. Every step forward is an achievement worth acknowledging. Keep going, knowing that each day brings you closer to your dreams.

July 11

Hope is a mindset. It's choosing to believe that no matter how difficult things are now, they won't stay that way forever. Embrace hope as a daily practice, and let it uplift your spirit.

July 12

Fearlessness means letting go of what others think. Don't let the fear of judgment or criticism hold you back from pursuing what you want. Be bold enough to live life on your own terms.

July 13

Motivation doesn't come from waiting; it comes from doing. Take action today, even if it's small. The act of moving forward will reignite your passion and keep you focused on the bigger picture.

July 14

Hope is the fuel that keeps you going in the face of adversity. When setbacks arise, stay hopeful by remembering that every challenge is temporary, and better days are always ahead.

July 15

I release the fear of judgment and embrace my authenticity. I am fearless in being exactly who I am, without apology.

July 16

I am brave enough to take risks and try new things. I trust that every step I take brings me closer to becoming my best self.

July 17

I step into my power with fearlessness. I no longer shrink to fit in; instead, I rise to stand at my full potential.

July 18

Fearlessness isn't about eliminating fear; it's about being brave enough to pursue your dreams despite it. Acknowledge your fears but move forward anyway, knowing that courage grows with each bold step.

July 19

Being a fearless leader means embracing change, uncertainty, and challenge. I know that growth and innovation come from stepping outside of my comfort zone.

July 20

Hope is an active choice. When things get tough, choose hope over despair. It may not always be easy, but hope gives you the strength to keep going when the road ahead is uncertain.

July 21

Fearlessness means being willing to take risks. You'll never know what's possible until you try. Take a leap of faith today, knowing that the greatest growth often comes from the boldest moves.

July 22

Motivation comes from consistency. Stay committed to your goals by showing up every day, even when you don't feel like it. The key to success is to stay consistent in your efforts.

July 23

Fearlessness in leadership is about trust—trusting my team, my intuition, and the process. Together, we can achieve greatness, one brave step at a time.

July 24

Fearlessness requires embracing uncertainty. Life is unpredictable, but that's where the magic happens. Step into the unknown with confidence, trusting that you are capable of handling whatever comes your way.

July 25

Great leaders are not fearless; they lead in spite of their fears. I embrace my fears, using them as stepping stones to become a stronger, more compassionate leader.

July 26

Hope is a form of resilience. It's choosing to stay positive and forward-thinking, even when faced with challenges. Nurture hope today by focusing on the possibilities rather than the limitations.

July 27

Fearlessness is about taking the first step, even when you're unsure of the outcome. Be brave enough to try something new today, trusting that every step you take leads to growth.

July 28

Motivation is fueled by belief in yourself. Trust that you are capable of achieving your goals, and let that belief drive you forward. The more you believe in yourself, the more motivated you'll feel.

July 29

Hope turns dreams into reality. Stay hopeful by visualizing the future you want and take action each day to move closer to that vision. Hope fuels progress.

July 30

Fearlessness means trusting your instincts. You know what's best for you, so trust yourself enough to follow your gut. Be bold in your decisions and fearless in pursuing what feels right.

July 31

As this month comes to an end, reflect on how far you've come in developing motivation, hope, and fearlessness. Carry these qualities forward into the next month, knowing that your journey is just beginning.

End-of-the-Month Reflection

As July comes to an end, let us remind ourselves that fear is just a feeling that takes over and prevents us from taking real chances in life. The existence of fear prevents us from reaching our full potential because we are so worried about failure. Do not be afraid to try new things, make new friends, travel to new places, speak up, advocate for others, and be yourself. You are not being your authentic self if you keep holding back. Try something new tomorrow. So what if you fail? You can finally check it off your bucket list.

August

The Month of Embracing Change, Loss, and Resilience

August is a month of transition. It's a time when the seasons begin to shift, symbolizing the changes we often face in our own lives. This month, we focus on navigating loss, embracing change, and building resilience. Loss, in any form, whether it's the passing of a loved one, the end of a relationship, or the closing of a chapter, leaves a void that can feel overwhelming. Yet in the midst of grief, there is an opportunity to grow, to adapt, and to find strength in the midst of sorrow.

Life is full of inevitable losses, and while we cannot avoid them, we can control how we respond to them. Grief takes time, and it is not a linear journey. However, by embracing the emotions, accepting the changes, and allowing ourselves the space to heal, we can emerge stronger and more resilient. This month is about allowing yourself to feel the pain, honoring the memories, and learning to move forward without forgetting what was left behind.

Personal Reflection: Navigating Loss and Finding Strength

Loss is one of the hardest parts of life. Whether it's losing a loved one, a job, or even a sense of security, each loss feels like a piece of our world has been taken away, leaving us feeling incomplete. Like many of you, I have lost a lot of things in this life but the worse is to lose a loved one shockingly and unfortunately, I have faced that type of loss more than once. In 1992, when my brother Henneh drowned, I thought that was the worst pain until August 2020, when we lost our older sister, Jemi, suddenly.

I remember our last call and I replay it daily, wishing it would end differently. I had spoken with Jemi that morning, but she was rushing to go house hunting with Lilah, our other sister, and as usual, she was running behind so it was rather brief. She had promised to call later. I talk to my siblings almost every day even though we all lived in different states at the time, but Jemi was the one sibling I talked to at least three times a day.

Later that night, I was in the shower when my husband barged in. He had a worried look on his face, and my brother-in-law who was staying with us at the time was now standing in our bedroom—I could hear his voice. One of them—I cannot remember which one—said, "Jemi has been rushed to the hospital." My heart almost stopped beating. This had to be serious because Jemi hated hospitals, so I knew it was bad. My phone rang, interrupting my confused state of mind. It was Jemi on the other line. To be honest, she sounded normal—calm but distant. She did not sound afraid but rather resolute. Our conversation was brief because she wanted me to know that she was in an ICU at a hospital in Michigan and might be taken into surgery soon. I did not ask what was going on. I was too confused and scared to get any more details.

She did most of the talking, "Annise, I am at the hospital." Silence. "I think I am going to die." More silence. "Please don't forget about Karina." I don't know why but it felt eerily final even though she sounded normal. I recall only being able to say, "OK, OK, OK. Stop talking. Karina is fine, and you will be fine. I love you." And that was our final call. She had to go; they did not want her on the phone. That was it.

I will forever be grateful that my last words to my older sister were "I love you." I think we should always try to leave people with loving words or a positive memory because we just never know if there will be another opportunity. Jemi went into surgery the next day and never came out—the worst day of my life. I still cry every night. She was my best friend.

The loss of a sibling is a profound, life-altering experience. Your sibling is often your first friend, your longest companion, and the person who shares your earliest memories. When that bond is broken, it can feel as though a part of you is gone as well. While every loss is painful, grieving a sibling carries its own unique challenges. For me, loss has often felt like the ground being pulled from beneath my feet, leaving me searching for balance and stability once again. What I've learned over time, though, is that grief doesn't have a set timeline. There's no right way to mourn, no perfect way to move on. The heart doesn't operate on a schedule, and each wave of emotion is a reminder that the bond shared was meaningful. In the midst of grief, I've found solace in small moments—remembering the laughter shared, reflecting on the lessons learned, and accepting that it's OK to feel vulnerable and broken for a while.

I've had to remind myself that loss, though painful, can also teach us resilience. With every tear, there's strength being built. We don't have to be strong every day, but in those moments when we feel our weakest, we often find that we're stronger than we ever knew. And sometimes, it's not about bouncing back to who we were before the loss, but about growing into a new version of ourselves who carries the experience with grace and strength.

The journey through loss is not about "getting over it" but rather learning how to carry it with you in a way that honors the memory, and the love shared. Loss changes us, but it doesn't have to break us. There is beauty in the cracks, and through these cracks, light can shine again. For me, this is a reminder that it's OK to mourn, take time to heal, and be gentle with yourself as you learn to live with the change.

Daily Affirmations

August 1

I give myself permission to grieve in my own time and my own way, knowing that healing is a journey.

August 2

Today, I honor the love and memories that remain, and I trust that the pain I feel will soften with time.

August 3

Each day, I am finding the strength to face my loss and to keep moving forward, even if the steps are small.

August 4

I acknowledge my feelings of sadness, and I allow myself to process them without judgment.

August 5

Loss is a part of life, but so is healing. I trust that I will emerge from this experience stronger and more resilient.

August 6

I will carry the love and memories with me, knowing that they will always be a part of who I am.

August 7

I am gentle with myself today, allowing space for both grief and hope to coexist.

August 8

Though I feel the weight of loss, I also feel the support of those around me, helping me through this journey.

August 9

I trust that in time, the pain will lessen, and I will find peace in the memories I cherish.

August 10

I am allowed to feel joy again, even in the midst of loss. I know that healing comes in waves, and that's OK.

August 11

Today, I choose to honor my emotions and to give myself grace as I navigate this difficult time.

August 12

I am strong enough to carry the weight of my loss while still moving forward with hope.

August 13

I trust that the process of healing will unfold in its own time, and I am patient with myself.

August 14

Though loss has changed me, I am learning to adapt and grow through the pain.

August 15

I give myself permission to laugh, to smile, and to enjoy life again, knowing that it doesn't diminish the love I feel.

August 16

Each day, I am taking steps toward healing, even when the progress feels slow.

August 17

I release the guilt of moving forward, knowing that healing is not about forgetting but about learning to live with the change.

August 18

I am surrounded by love and support, even when I feel alone in my grief.

August 19

I trust that time will bring clarity and peace, and I allow myself to embrace the healing journey.

August 20

Today, I focus on the moments of light in my life, knowing that joy can exist even in times of sorrow.

August 21

I accept that grief is not linear, and I allow myself to feel all the emotions that come with loss.

August 22

I choose to honor the love that was shared, and I trust that it will continue to guide me as I heal.

August 23

I know that I am resilient, and I will find my way through this loss, one step at a time.

August 24

I give myself permission to rest, to breathe, and to take care of myself during this time of grief.

August 25

Though I carry the weight of loss, I also carry the strength to keep moving forward.

August 26

I am patient with my healing, knowing that it will take time, and that's OK.

August 27

Today, I choose to focus on the love and light that remain, even in the midst of sadness.

August 28

I trust that each day brings me closer to peace, and I allow myself the time and space to heal.

August 29

I am learning to live with the loss, knowing that the love shared will always be a part of me.

August 30

Though loss has changed my life, it will not define my future. I am strong enough to create new chapters.

August 31

As this month comes to an end, I honor the journey of grief and the resilience I have built along the way.

End-of-Month Reflection

As August comes to a close, reflect on the ways in which you have faced your loss, navigated your grief, and begun to heal. Each step, no matter how small, has brought you closer to a place of acceptance and peace. The journey through loss is never easy, but it is one that teaches us about strength, resilience, and the capacity to keep going, even when it feels impossible. As you move forward, carry with you the lessons learned and the love that remains, knowing that you are stronger for having faced the challenge. Embrace the hope that, in time, light will return, and you will continue to grow through every season of life.

September

The Month Of Rebuilding And Embracing Destiny

September symbolizes a time of rebuilding what has been lost or broken, restoring balance, strength, and a sense of self. Whether you're rebuilding after a personal setback, re-energizing your goals, or reawakening relationships, this month invites you to focus on piecing things back together, finding your happiness, and embracing the belief that while our lives may be pre-ordained, we still have the power to shape our journey.

PERSONAL REFLECTION: SHIFTING SPACES:

Rebuilding isn't about starting from scratch; it's about starting from experience. When life shakes us to our core—whether through loss, disappointment, or unexpected challenges—we are given an opportunity to rebuild with intention and purpose. This process is difficult, but it's a necessary part of growth.

There have been times when I felt as if I'd lost everything, and the idea of moving forward seemed impossible. But, as the days passed, I found small pieces of myself to restore, one by one. Rebuilding wasn't about returning to who I once was, but embracing the new version of myself. That meant embracing my new single life in a downsized luxury apartment.

I went from owning a 5,000 sq. ft. single-family home in the suburbs to renting a 1,600 sq. ft. apartment in the city. At first, the adjustment felt overwhelming, but over time, I grew to love it. Our minds adapt so quickly. I embraced a minimalist lifestyle—simple, manageable, and carefree. I had just one bill, everything included, which meant more money for shoes I sometimes forgot I owned. No trash to take out, no dry cleaning to worry about, since everything was inside my lovely Rockville apartment—life was easy.

I'd settled into my single life after the kids left, and it was starting to feel really good. I didn't have a cat or a dog, and even the plant I tried to grow didn't last long - I've never had a green thumb, but I tried – I really tried but alas. At the end of the day, it was just me and the birds that perched on my quaint veranda overlooking the pool house and even stared at me sometimes. I suspect they must have seen me dance nonstop some days because why the rude stare. As for food, since I had no kids or husband then, I had Panera's Greek salad with grilled chicken for dinner almost every night. It became such a habit that the servers knew my order as soon as I walked in. Then, I'd return to my apartment, binge-watch the news, dance around until I got dizzy, and go to bed with no care in the world.

But just when I thought I had settled into my new life, God decided it was time for me to be a wife again. Really God!!! I was shocked by this detour, but I had to trust that it was part of my journey. So, I obeyed and remarried—much to the surprise of many. And now, I had some real problems…sharing my closet space with a man who had more clothes and definitely more shoes than me. Didn't even know that was possible but he did arrive from London with suitcases of shoes and they were all in their actual shoe boxes. As you can all imagine, my apartment closet was never going to be able to house the collection of two fashionistas and that exactly how I had to convert from being a minimalist to a homeowner again…a twist I did not see coming.

This is proof that even though we hold the pen to write our own chapters, destiny may outline certain frameworks of our lives although it does not dictate every detail. However, it is important that whilst destiny does play a role in our lives, we are not powerless – we can still influence how we respond to detours in life. One thing that we do not have to do is to wait for destiny to give us the green light for our inner peace. Our decisions, attitudes, and resilience all shape our experiences profoundly and help us create that inner feeling. If we are chaotic, then it will be difficult to find peace but if we practice calmness, patience, gratitude and kindness, we are on the right path to find peace.

I truly believe we have the power to control and change the trajectory of situations, especially those that directly impact our happiness. In life's journey, we all seek peace and happiness, and these are two things we should never convince ourselves are out of our control or put in the hands of others. No matter how much we believe our lives are pre-ordained, always remember: Happiness is an inside job. It is completely up to you whether you choose happiness or self-pity and internal chaos. The choice is yours.

Rebuilding and Restoring

I stand amidst the ruins,
Of all that once was whole,
Each piece a silent story,
A crack that feeds my soul.

Rebuilding takes some time,
It's hard, but worth the fight,
I gather up the pieces,
And search for inner light.

I seek not perfect endings,
But growth through every test,
In mending what was fractured,
I find my truest rest.

Each step is made with courage,
Each loss becomes my guide,
As I rebuild my spirit,
With strength I cannot hide.

—Annise

Daily Affirmations

September 1

I am enough – I know my worth – I love myself.

September 2

Change is good and I embrace the new me.

September 3

I am confident that my new path will lead me to happier days.

September 4

Each step I take in rebuilding is a step toward becoming the person I am meant to be.

September 5

I trust the process, knowing that every challenge I face shapes my journey.

September 6

Rebuilding is a journey, not a destination. I trust that each day brings me closer to my purpose.

September 7

I trust in my ability to rebuild, even when the path ahead is unclear.

September 8

I am worthy of the life I am creating, and I trust that everything will fall into place.

September 9

I am not afraid of change, because I know it will lead me to a better me.

September 10

I am strong enough to face whatever comes my way, knowing that it is part of my destiny.

September 11

I will enjoy this process of rebuilding even on my darkest days because it part of my becoming.

September 12

I am creating a life filled with purpose, joy, and meaning with every action I take.

September 13

I release fear and embrace the unknown, trusting that it is leading me to where I need to be.

September 14

My destiny is mine to create. I have the power to shape my future with each choice I make.

September 15

I am not afraid to fall or fumble – I am not perfect.

September 16

I will not wait on others to bring me joy – I will find joy in everything I undertake.

September 17

I will strive to see only the lessons in my journey accepting that it is ok to fall but I will rise again.

September 18

I know that this process will not be easy but I am resilient in my quest of inner peace so I will focus on my goals and accept every fall as a lesson.

September 19

I have big dreams, and I know that if I stay focused it will all come into fruition.

September 20

I embrace the unknown, knowing that it holds the keys to my future.

Scptcmbcr 21

I trust that every new step I take is aligned with my highest good.

September 22

I am creating a life full of purpose, clarity, and joy, and I embrace every part of it.

September 23

I am in the process of becoming the best version of myself, and I trust the journey.

September 24

I have everything I need to rebuild, I just need to be patient and stay the course.

September 25

I embrace my destiny with grace.

September 26

I forgive myself for all my failed attempts – I will not give up.

September 27

I will accept all the new challenges coming my way as a challenge to growth.

September 28

I am blessed and know that my God is watching over me.

September 29

Today I will dance and rejoice - there is always something to be happy about.

September 30

I am grateful – I am thankful for every challenge, every lesson and for every gain.

September End-of-Month Reflection: Rebuilding and Embracing Destiny

As September draws to a close, I reflect not only on the progress I've made but also on the strength and resilience that have emerged throughout this journey. Rebuilding is not just about recovering what was lost; it's about reimagining, transforming, and creating something far more meaningful. It's a journey of rediscovery and evolution, one that reminds me that I have the ability to adapt, grow, and become stronger with each new challenge.

I've learned that rebuilding doesn't have to be linear. Sometimes, we find ourselves at a point where we believe we've reached the peak—our career, family, and health aligned perfectly. But life has a way of throwing unexpected challenges at us, and we must learn to start again, armed with the experience we've gained. We may feel as though we've already won the race, only to realize that it's not over. These moments, when life forces us to revisit old wounds, provide us with a powerful choice: we can either see them as setbacks or embrace them as lessons to move forward with purpose.

This month has been a time of deep reflection and healing. I've acknowledged old wounds and faced the parts of myself that needed attention. I've allowed myself to embrace the discomfort of change and release habits, relationships, and even mindsets that no longer serve me. Through each challenge, I've found opportunities to rebuild with intention. I've focused on creating a stronger foundation of self-compassion, courage, and patience. I have come to accept that sometimes, I just need to be with myself – I am enough. "You are enough."

The process of rebuilding has also taught me something profound: healing isn't always about returning to a former state. It's about embracing the evolution that comes with each experience, the shifts that lead me closer to who I'm meant to be and truly understanding who I am am. As I've rebuilt, I've embraced the idea that each step forward, no matter how small, is part of the larger picture of aligning my life with my true destiny. I've learned to trust that the discomfort of transformation will eventually reveal a version of me that is more authentic.

One of the most powerful lessons I've learned is that we are not powerless in the face of life's detours. While destiny certainly plays a role in shaping our lives, we have the power to influence how we respond to the unexpected. Even though life may push us into unfamiliar spaces, we are capable of choosing how we rebuild, how we embrace change, and how we move forward.

This month, I have focused on embracing the shifts in my life and trusting that every change, every challenge, and every unexpected turn is part of a bigger plan. I've come to understand that rebuilding isn't just about fixing what's broken; it's about creating something new—something that aligns with my highest purpose and my truest self.

As I move forward into the next month, I carry with me the strength I've gained, the lessons I've learned, and the hope that every step of rebuilding takes me closer to my life's goals. I am a new woman now as I enter the next chapter.

October

The Month of Gratitude and Compassion

Thank you. These two simple words mean so much when said to someone in a meaningful way. I am not referring to the thank you that is said out of obligation. I am referring to the one that comes from the heart and is sincere. It shows our appreciation and gratitude for a kind deed, and this should never be reserved for only big favors, accomplishments, or special occasions. In fact, I have come to realize that gratitude is most powerful in the small, everyday moments. It is the little things in life that really bring us complete joy—a gentle reminder that I am alive—like feeling the sun on my face, the smile of a mere stranger as we stand in the checkout line, a call from an old friend, or a nice compliment from your spouse. All these are moments we should be thankful for and never take for granted.

Compassion, too, has been a transformative force in my life. I've learned that it's easy to be compassionate toward others, but true growth comes when we turn that compassion inward. Often, we are our own harshest critics, holding ourselves to impossible standards. But when we approach ourselves with the same kindness, we offer others, we create space for healing and growth. It is important to show ourselves the same gratitude and compassion we give to others; this is self-love.

I make it a habit to remind myself that gratitude is a daily practice, not a fleeting emotion. I commit to finding something each day to be thankful for, no matter how small. And I make compassion a cornerstone of my interactions—listening more intently, judging less, and being more patient with myself and others. This shift in perspective has allowed me to experience life with more contentment and joy, regardless of the circumstances.

Personal Reflection: We All Need Grace

Learning patience has been a journey, and I'm proud of the progress I've made. There was a time when I would feel an immediate sense of irritation if someone took too long to get to the point of their story or if they struggled with tasks that seemed simple to me. In these moments, I could feel my impatience rise, creating tension in situations where understanding and empathy were needed. I realized that my own expectations for efficiency and clarity didn't always align with others' natural pace or approach, and I struggled to see that diversity as valuable.

As time went on, I became more aware of how my impatience was affecting not only my relationships but also my ability to appreciate other perspectives. I started to actively remind myself that everyone has a unique way of processing and presenting information, each bringing their own strengths to the table. Gradually, I learned to let go of the need to control the pace or outcome and instead began focusing on listening—really listening—not just to the words but to the intent and emotions behind them.

This shift wasn't immediate or easy. It took an intentional effort to step back and allow others the space to express themselves freely. I practiced patience with myself in this learning process as well, understanding that my urge to rush wasn't a flaw but simply a pattern I needed to rewire. Over time, I grew to value the diversity in how we communicate and work, recognizing that a variety of styles and approaches only enrich our shared experiences. This lesson in patience has shown me that there's wisdom in slowing down, allowing others their space, and realizing that one size truly does not fit all.

Compassion, though, has always been a value I tried to live by, but one particular experience deepened my understanding of its true power. A few years ago, I was going through a challenging time at work. I had a colleague who seemed to undermine my efforts at every turn. There was tension between us, and I began to harbor feelings of resentment. I felt like I was being unfairly targeted, and it left me stressed and disheartened.

One day, after a particularly difficult meeting where I felt my contributions were dismissed, I found myself fuming on the drive home. My mind was filled with frustration, and I kept replaying the moment over and over again. That evening, as I sat with my thoughts, something shifted within me. I had spent a lot of time trying to figure out what my colleague had against me but it came up empty each time and it made me rethink my mindset. Maybe it wasn't me. What if it was nothing personal? What if they did not even realize the pain and hurt they were putting me through because they were in such a sunken place? Maybe they were struggling with something I couldn't see. Maybe their actions had more to do with their own inner battles than with me.

The next day, I decided to view this ongoing problem from a different perspective – what if this really had nothing to do with me? And so, I approached the situation with compassion. I invited them to lunch, hoping to open the door for a friendly discussion. Over that meal, I expressed how I felt they were constantly undermining all my efforts without giving constructive feedback and how much they affected me mentally. To my surprise, my colleague was unaware of the emotional damage and perhaps even the career damage their actions had caused me. I discovered that they were going through a difficult personal crisis—one that had been weighing heavily on them. The stress they were feeling had unintentionally spilled over into their professional life. At the end of that meal, I learnt more about that colleague in that short time than I knew working closely with them for nearly five years. And when they said "thank you for taking the time and not judging me" almost teary-eyed, that truly made me feel as if I had saved a life. It was like they had been hoping that someone will notice and provide them a safe space to be vulnerable. Never doubt the power of compassion and always refrain from judging.

At that moment, my resentment melted away. I saw them not as an adversary, but as a person carrying burdens of their own. This didn't excuse their past behavior, but it gave me the clarity to see beyond my own frustrations. Compassion allowed me to extend grace, not only for them but for myself. It softened the edges of my anger and helped me find a way forward, both in our working relationship and in how I approach conflict in general.

I've also learned that offering grace is a reflection of my own humility. Just as I desire grace when I stumble, I must be willing to extend it to others. Humility builds teams, strengthens relationships, and fosters a sense of unity. By being humble and offering grace, we create an environment where people feel seen, valued, and supported—a space where growth and collaboration can thrive.

That experience taught me that compassion isn't just a nice ideal; it's a powerful tool for building connections, resolving conflict, and finding peace within ourselves. By choosing to see humanity in others, even when they hurt or disappoint us, we create opportunities for healing and growth.

Daily Affirmations

October 1

Today, I begin with a heart full of gratitude. I choose to focus on the blessings in my life, both big and small.

October 2

Compassion begins with me. I will be kind to myself and extend that kindness to others.

October 3

Gratitude transforms my perspective. I choose to see the good in every situation.

October 4

I offer compassion without judgment, knowing that everyone is on their own journey.

October 5

I am grateful for the lessons that life has taught me. Every experience has made me stronger.

October 6

Compassion is my superpower. I will uplift others with my words and actions.

October 7

I choose gratitude as my daily mindset. It brings me peace and joy in every moment.

October 8

Today, I will show myself the same compassion I show others. I deserve kindness too.

October 9

Gratitude helps me focus on abundance. I am thankful for everything I have and everything I am.

October 10

I approach challenges with compassion, knowing that each one brings an opportunity to grow.

October 11

My heart is filled with gratitude. I acknowledge all the beauty in my life.

October 12

Compassion creates connection. I will approach others with understanding and empathy.

October 13

Gratitude is a magnet for joy. The more I practice it, the more blessings I attract.

October 14

I will not judge myself harshly today. I choose to be compassionate and forgiving toward myself.

October 15

Today, I will offer gratitude for the present moment, appreciating exactly where I am.

October 16

Compassion makes me stronger. By uplifting others, I uplift myself.

October 17

I am thankful for the opportunities I've been given, and I will make the most of them.

October 18

With compassion, I can face any challenge. I trust in my ability to navigate life with grace.

October 19

I choose to see the good in myself and others. Gratitude opens my eyes to the beauty all around me.

October 20

Compassion softens my heart. Today, I will be gentle with myself and those I encounter.

October 21

I am grateful for this journey. Every step I take is a step toward growth.

October 22

Today, I will show up with compassion and empathy, knowing that everyone I meet has their own struggles.

October 23

I trust in the power of gratitude to shift my perspective and bring more joy into my life.

October 24

Compassion is a gift I give freely, without expectation. It nurtures the soul.

October 25

I will find something to be grateful for today, even in the smallest moments.

October 26

I release judgment and replace it with compassion. I am gentle with myself and others.

October 27

Gratitude fills my heart with peace. I will carry this peace with me throughout the day.

October 28

I am compassionate in my words, my actions, and my thoughts. I will spread kindness wherever I go.

October 29

Today, I will reflect on all that I am grateful for, knowing that appreciation is the foundation of happiness.

October 30

Compassion deepens my relationships. I will connect with others through understanding and love.

October 31

As this month ends, I reflect on all the moments of gratitude and compassion I've experienced. I carry these lessons with me as I move forward.

End-of-the-Month Reflection

As October draws to a close, I find myself reflecting on the lessons of patience, gratitude, and compassion. This month has been a journey of learning to slow down, appreciate the present, and approach both myself and others with understanding and empathy. Developing patience has been a reminder that not everything needs to happen on my timeline. Sometimes, the greatest growth comes when we allow life to unfold in its own time, trusting the process and releasing the urge to control every outcome. I really had to train my mind to do that because being patient was not my strongest trait. However, in my personal journey to become a better version of myself and to allow myself to show empathy to others, I realize that gratitude and compassion go hand-in-hand with patience.

Gratitude has deepened my appreciation for the small but significant moments in life. It has reminded me to honor progress—even when it's incremental—and to celebrate resilience in myself and others. Each experience, each interaction, has become an opportunity to be thankful and to recognize the blessings that exist even amidst challenges. Gratitude has grounded me, helping me to stay connected to what truly matters, even when life feels uncertain. I only need to look around and see all the goodness around me and be thankful rather than focus on what has failed and play victim or throw myself a pity party. I am not suggesting that you ignore your pain or loss during these times. Show yourself compassion but still be grateful in that space.

Compassion has been a guide, teaching me to look beyond the surface frustrations and see the humanity in everyone I encounter. By choosing compassion, I've found a way to approach conflicts with a softer heart, recognizing that everyone is on their own journey, often carrying unseen burdens. Together, these qualities have shaped my October, creating a foundation of peace, understanding, and inner strength that I carry forward. I close this month with a heart more open, a more resilient spirit, and a deeper commitment to living each day with patience, gratitude, and compassion.

November

The Month of Purpose, Positive Intentions, and Connections

November invites a deepened sense of purpose, a time to reflect, realign, and cultivate intentional connections that uplift and inspire. It is a month for tuning into what truly matters, stripping away distractions, and centering yourself around your core values and life's true calling.

This month is about aligning your actions with your purpose, setting clear and positive intentions, and fostering meaningful relationships that support your growth. It's not just about external success, but about nurturing inner peace, cultivating wisdom, and embracing a life of balance and self-awareness.

In November, allow yourself the space to listen to your inner voice. Reflect on your journey, evaluate what serves you, and let go of what holds you back. Strengthen your connections—whether with yourself or others—by engaging more deeply and authentically. Through purposeful actions, clear intentions, and meaningful relationships, you can live more fully, embrace your path, and move closer to your highest potential.

Personal Reflection: Realignment and Rediscovery—A Journey of Intentionality

November has always felt like a month of quiet transition, a time when I pause to recalibrate before the year ends. It's a season for deeper reflection where I assess how well my actions align with my purpose and whether my life mirrors the values I hold close. With the year drawing to a close, November serves as a checkpoint and a reminder to strip away the noise, refocus on what truly matters, and let go of anything that no longer serves me. Do I always stick to the plan? No! But at least I try to make some alterations in my life. As humans, we are not perfect, but we fail ourselves when we stop trying to hold ourselves accountable. We must set timelines and self-performance reviews just like you would with your career.

This past November felt different. I decided to embark on a journey back to Sierra Leone, my homeland—a place I hadn't visited in over a decade. The decision wasn't just about returning to familiar surroundings; it was about rediscovering parts of myself that had become dormant. It was an intentional trip, filled with the purpose of reconnecting with my roots, my volunteer work, and old friendships. Sierra Leone isn't just a location; it's the place that raised me, shaped me, and still holds a piece of my heart.

Going into this trip, I knew I was not even close to the woman I wanted to be or the legacy I would love to leave behind, so I was mindful about dropping habits that were clearly not serving me and focusing on cultivating peace and self-care. I moved through this period with a sense of clarity, knowing what I wanted to embrace in my life and what I needed to let go of but also acknowledging that I was not yet there. The journey was more about self-connection and finding my real purpose. From the outside, it may appear like some sort of fun vacation but this journey will forever change my life.

In many ways, November reminded me that finding purpose is an ongoing process. It requires regular self-reflection, setting clear intentions, and surrounding ourselves with people and practices that nurture our growth. My trip to Sierra Leone was a beautiful reminder of the importance of staying grounded in purpose, being intentional about my actions, and fostering meaningful connections—both new and old.

Most people see me as an extrovert, but I am only that when I am in public. I actually prefer to spend more time with myself—this revelation will shock anyone who knows me, but it is a true confession. Perhaps, you can say I am an ambivert and my trip back home confirmed this. I had no kids, husband, or siblings to care for so my only real responsibility was finding the *real* Annise. I spent a lot of time just sitting at Lumley Beach - it became my sanctuary—where the sounds of the sea acted as a balm for my soul, allowing me to sit with my thoughts, write, and reflect. There, on the sands of my youth, I began to piece together not only this reflection but parts of myself that I had forgotten. It was as if I was rewriting my own story with a sense of purpose, clarity, and compassion for myself.

I couldn't help but feel a deep sense of gratitude for the beauty of my homeland, yet sadness for the stark contrasts I witnessed. Freetown, with its breathtaking landscapes, also carries the weight of poverty, corruption, and suffering. The streets that once brought me joy as a young girl were now filled with heartbreaking scenes. They did not even look familiar anymore. They are now crowded and filled with street vendors, *okadas* (the country's main source of transportation), and traffic that hardly moves. The beach strip is another tale. It is common to see young women or girls, indecently clad, walking aimlessly at night, clearly selling their bodies, and young men, victims of drugs, lost in a haze. It was a sobering reminder of how much work remains to be done. I did not recognize this country but there was no love lost either.

I was mad about not doing more for my own country and berated myself quietly for becoming one of those who only complained and never took action. At times, I was embarrassed at my non-action. Why had I not done more for my country? Why had I not visited more? Why are we so complacent as a nation? It was a difficult realization to sit with—the discomfort of knowing that the country has so many resources that could make it a coveted tourist destination yet we are only known as one of the poorest countries in the world really troubled my soul. Are we that cursed with bad leaders or are we just an irresponsible nation? Is God mad at us? Why Salone, why? Like many of my Sierra Leonean friends from the diaspora, I had a thousand questions running across my mind as I sat on that beach. So many beautiful memories were now overtaken by the stark difference of my reality and I couldn't help but feel powerless and a sense of shame and betrayal to my own country. The weight of this realization was heavy, but it was also a call to action. I knew that this trip wasn't just about nostalgia; it was about reigniting a fire within me to do more, to serve with a renewed sense of purpose.

And yet, amid the frustration and reflection, I found a sense of hope. I reconnected with friends and made new ones, each connection reminding me of the power of human relationships. In those moments, I felt a deepened sense of purpose that had been missing for so long. I realized that sometimes, we have to go back to our roots to move forward. Sierra Leone has given me not only my identity but also a renewed sense of direction. I owe this place.

November, for me, was about shedding the layers of complacency and reconnecting with my values. It was about aligning my intentions with my actions, being purposeful in my decisions, and making connections that nurtured my spirit. In many ways, my trip home was the beginning of a new chapter, one where I am more intentional about my legacy, more compassionate with myself, and more determined to make a meaningful difference in the world around me no matter how small.

As I move forward, I hold on to the lessons November taught me—that purpose is not stagnant but something we must continually refine; that intention is a powerful force, guiding us toward what truly matters; and that connection—whether to people, places, or causes—is what gives our lives meaning. I now carry these lessons with me, knowing that my journey of self-discovery and purpose is far from over.

Daily Affirmations

November 1

Purpose begins with clarity. Start this month by reflecting on what truly matters to you. What are your deepest goals and values? Align your actions with your purpose and let them guide you through every decision.

November 2

My purpose guides me. I am intentional in all that I do, trusting that each step is aligned with my greater vision.

November 3

Connection is a source of strength. Reach out to someone today and engage in a meaningful conversation. Deep connections with others enrich your life and remind you that you are not alone on this journey.

November 4

Purpose gives you direction. When you're feeling lost or unsure, reconnect with your sense of purpose. Remind yourself why you started and let your purpose be the compass that guides you forward.

November 5

My journey is unique. I honor my path, embracing both the lessons and blessings along the way.

November 6

Connection requires vulnerability. I am learning to open up and share my authentic self. I will let go of the fear of judgment and embrace the beauty of real, honest communication.

November 7

Purpose isn't something you find; it's something you create. Every day, through your choices and actions, you are shaping your purpose. Be intentional about how you spend your time and energy.

November 8

Today, I dedicate time to self-care. I nourish my body, mind, and spirit, knowing that my well-being is my priority.

November 9

Connection is about presence. I will be fully present, not distracted and not thinking of the next task. True connection happens when you give your full attention to the moment.

November 10

My purpose is fueled by passion. I will reignite my passion by engaging in activities that bring me joy and fulfillment. When you love what you do, your sense of purpose grows stronger.

November 11

I trust in my ability to create meaningful connections that uplift and inspire me.

November 12

Today, I will take time to listen deeply to someone without offering advice or judgment. Empathy allows you to understand others on a deeper level and fosters stronger relationships.

November 13

Purpose gives meaning to your efforts. When you're clear on your purpose, the hard work feels worth it. Stay focused on the bigger picture and let your sense of purpose drive you through challenges.

November 14

Wisdom grows through self-reflection. Spend time today looking back on your experiences. What lessons have you learned from your past that can help you navigate your future?

November 15

Connection is nurtured by kindness. A simple act of kindness today can strengthen the bonds you have with others. Whether it's a kind word or a helping hand, small gestures make a big impact.

November 16

Purpose brings fulfillment. Today, I will reflect on how my actions and choices align with my deeper purpose and make adjustments where needed.

November 17

I am grateful for my connections, both old and new. They remind me of my roots and inspire me to grow.

November 18

Connection is built on trust. I will not make promises that I cannot keep and do my best to become a more trustworthy, reliable, and compassionate friend. Trust is the foundation of meaningful relationships.

November 19

Purpose evolves over time. Don't be afraid to revisit your goals and adjust them as you grow. Your purpose isn't fixed. It changes as you gain more clarity and experience in life.

November 20

Wisdom means knowing when to act and when to wait. Some decisions require immediate action, while others need time to unfold. Trust your intuition to guide you in making wise choices.

November 21

I know that connection requires effort and that relationships don't thrive on autopilot. I will be intentional about nurturing connections with others. I will take time to invest in my friendships, family, and community.

November 22

I will be resilient when things get tough. I will allow my sense of purpose to be the strength that carries me through difficult times instead of letting my fears lead.

November 23

I am committed to living a life that reflects my highest values and intentions.

November 24

I know connection fosters joy so today, I will try to connect with others in meaningful ways. I will be present and not distracted.

November 25

I invest in my well-being by surrounding myself with positive influences and nurturing relationships.

November 26

Today, I reflect on my journey and celebrate the connections I've made, the lessons I've learned, and the person I'm becoming.

November 27

I will take time today to express gratitude to those who have supported and encouraged me. I will acknowledge the people who make my life better, and let them know they're appreciated.

November 28

I am aligned with my highest self. I let go of distractions and focus on living a life of purpose, peace, and fulfillment.

November 29

I am grateful for the journey and the connections I've made. Each step has brought me closer to where I need to be.

November 30

I am intentional in my actions, choosing to move forward with positivity and purpose. Connection is an ongoing journey. Relationships require time, care, and attention. I will make an effort to show up for my loved ones and watch those connections grow stronger and more meaningful over time.

End-of-the-Month Reflection

As November draws to a close, take time to reflect on the connections you've made, the intentions you've set, and the purpose you've embraced. This month has been a journey of self-discovery, filled with moments of clarity and intentional growth. Celebrate the positive shifts you've experienced, whether they came through reconnecting with loved ones, releasing old habits, or deepening your sense of purpose. Carry these lessons forward, trusting that you are building a life of fulfillment, peace, and meaningful connection.

December

The Month of Reflection, Intentionality, and Authenticity

As the final month of the year, December provides a natural pause—a moment to reflect deeply on our journey and to assess how closely our actions align with our true selves. It's a time to honor authenticity, letting go of any masks we've worn and embracing who we genuinely are. Reflection is not just about revisiting the past, but about understanding how our experiences have shaped us and finding the courage to stand in our truth.

This month also encourages intentionality. As we prepare to transition into a new year, there's an opportunity to become more deliberate with our choices and to set clear intentions that reflect our deepest values and aspirations. Instead of rushing through this season, we can approach it with mindfulness, choosing to engage in the activities and relationships that truly matter.

December calls for us to live authentically, reflect meaningfully, and act with purpose. By focusing on who we are at our core and making intentional decisions, we close the year with clarity and set the stage for a new beginning rooted in honesty and purpose.

Personal Reflection: Life is Like a Game of Chess

As I reflect on this year, I am reminded that life, much like a game of chess, is a constant interplay of strategy, patience, and adaptability. Every decision we make, every move we choose, is significant, even the ones that seem small or inconsequential at the time. Chess teaches us that not every move is about immediate gain; sometimes, it's about setting up the board for what comes next, planning ahead, and thinking with intention.

In life, much like chess, I have faced moments where I've had to pause and reflect on my choices, realizing that certain paths, while difficult, were necessary for growth. There have been sacrifices, unexpected turns, and times when I felt backed into a corner, but with reflection comes clarity. I use my time in that corner not to feel sorry for myself but rather to understand how I got there and what lesson I can take from being in this place right now. I've learned to embrace these moments as opportunities to realign with my values and to act with more deliberate intention. Not once do I ever feel sorry for myself when things do not work out, when I find myself in a bad situation, or when things don't go as planned. In this space of intentionality, I have accepted that just like the game of chess, sometimes, moving too fast will only jeopardize every piece.

Recently, I was faced with a drawback. A person who refuses to see setbacks as blessings would have gone into depression if they found themselves in the same situation but I choose to see the light through the cracks in the darkness. Instead of recoiling into sadness, I accepted all the doors being shut in my face as the wrong ventures. I decided to sit back, re-evaluate what I thought was my well-put-together plan, create new ideas, try to see the lessons from my failed projects, and then devise a new plan—hopefully, a much better one this time.

This past year, I've focused on being more authentic, removing the layers of expectations from others, societal pressures, and even the masks I've worn to protect myself from judgment. It hasn't been easy, but learning to step fully into my truth has been liberating. It's like positioning my queen on the board—powerful yet vulnerable—knowing that each move forward carries weight and meaning.

Intentionality has also played a crucial role this year. I've realized that not every move has to be grand. Some of the most meaningful progress has come from subtle, thoughtful shifts. Whether it was spending more time with loved ones, making space for self-care, or reevaluating relationships and goals, the essence of moving with purpose has been a guiding force. Every action has been a deliberate step toward living a life that aligns with who I truly am, not just who I've been told to be.

As I close out this year, I look back on the lessons learned—both from the victories and the losses—and embrace the wisdom they've brought. Life may not always go according to plan, but like chess, it's about staying adaptable, adjusting your strategy, and moving forward with clarity. The key is to remain patient, intentional, and true to yourself, no matter how unpredictable the game may become.

In this month of reflection, I challenge myself and all of us to ask the following: Are we playing the game of life authentically with intentionality and purpose?

As we enter a new year, let's make our moves count, not just for the sake of winning, but for the fulfillment that comes with living our truth, even when the path is uncertain.

Reflections of This Year's Journey

As we welcome December; the end of the year,
We pause and reflect on what's been clear.
The paths we've walked, the lessons learned,
The fires kindled, the bridges burned.

With each step forward, each step back,
We found our way along the track.
In every choice, both bold and slight,
We sought the truth, we chased the light.

Intentions set with hearts sincere,
We lived with purpose, year by year.
Not every moment went as planned,
But still, we moved, we dare not stand.

And now we stand on this year's brink,
Reflecting on our journey's sync.
Our truth unmasked, our hearts aligned,
We step boldly forth – a new path defined.

To live with grace, to act with care,
To hold our joy, our love to share.
To move with purpose, clear and free,
Embracing all we're meant to be.

So as we close this year's last page,
And step into life's next stage—
With courage bold, and mindful hearts
We'll live our truth, and do our parts

—Annise

Daily Affirmations

December 1

Today, I embrace my journey with openness and gratitude. Each experience, each lesson, has brought me closer to my true self.

December 2

I honor my authenticity by letting go of expectations that no longer serve me. I am enough, just as I am.

December 3

My actions today are grounded in purpose. I choose to be intentional in my words, my thoughts, and my deeds.

December 4

Reflection brings clarity. I take time to look within and recognize how far I've come and the path I wish to take forward.

December 5

I am true to myself, embracing the unique qualities that make me who I am. I live each day with honesty and courage.

December 6

I give myself the grace to grow. Every step I take, no matter how small, leads me closer to my purpose.

December 7

Today, I choose to live mindfully, placing my focus only on what aligns with my values and brings me joy.

December 8

My actions are rooted in intention and clarity. I honor my goals by making deliberate choices that reflect my true desires.

December 9

I release any masks I've worn to protect myself. I trust that by being genuine, I attract the people and experiences meant for me.

December 10

Each day is an opportunity to be the truest version of myself. I commit to showing up as me, unapologetically.

December 11

Authenticity is my strength. I release the need for validation and trust that my path is uniquely mine.

December 12

I am grateful for every challenge, for they have taught me resilience, patience, and self-love.

December 13

Today, I let go of the past and open my heart to new beginnings. I am ready to step forward with purpose.

December 14

I embrace quiet moments of reflection, listening to the wisdom within. My inner voice is my guide.

December 15

I hold space for intentional rest, understanding that stillness is as valuable as action in my journey.

December 16

My strength lies in my authenticity, and I welcome opportunities to show my true colors.

December 17

I am intentional with my energy. Today, I choose to invest in what uplifts me and nurtures my spirit.

December 18

I trust in the unfolding of my journey, knowing that each day brings me closer to living my purpose.

December 19

I let go of perfection and embrace my true self. I am a work in progress, and that is enough.

December 20

My choices are a reflection of my values. I move forward with confidence, grounded in what matters most to me.

Dcccmbcr 21

Today, I make space for relationships that add depth and meaning to my life. I surround myself with authenticity and love.

December 22

I give thanks for all that I am and all that I am becoming. Each day, I move closer to the life I envision.

December 23

I honor my intentions by following through with integrity and persistence. My actions speak to who I am.

December 24

I release any self-doubt and replace it with self-trust. I have the wisdom and courage to navigate my path.

December 25

I am grateful for the present moment. In this season of giving, I remember to give kindness, compassion, and grace to myself.

December 26

My authenticity is a gift I offer to the world. I let go of any desire to fit a mold and embrace my unique light.

December 27

Today, I am grounded in intention. I choose to focus on what brings me peace and aligns with my purpose.

December 28

I give myself permission to rest, recharge, and prepare for new beginnings. Restoration is an essential part of my journey.

December 29

I am proud of the growth and healing I have achieved this year. I honor each step I've taken on my path.

December 30

I release anything that no longer serves me. I make space for abundance, joy, and positive change in the year to come.

December 31

I close this year with gratitude and an open heart. I am ready to step into the new year with purpose, authenticity, and love.

End-of-the-Month Reflectionw

As December draws to a close, I take this moment to reflect deeply on the journey of the past year. This month has encouraged me to live with intention, to let go of the superficial, and to embrace authenticity. In reviewing my experiences, I realize how each lesson, each setback, and each triumph has added depth and wisdom to my path. Life is not just a sequence of moments but a mosaic of intentional actions, choices made with purpose, and reflections that bring clarity.

Living with authenticity has empowered me to stand in my truth, no longer confined by the expectations of others. I am proud of the growth I've achieved, not because it's been perfect, but because it's been real and intentional. As I step into a new year, I carry forward this commitment to live purposefully, act with clarity, and honor the journey as it unfolds, knowing each step is part of a greater plan.

Looking Back, Moving Forward: The Final Prayer

As we reach the close of this book, it's my hope that each page has offered you strength, comfort, and insight. Life, in all its complexities, presents us with countless opportunities to reflect, rebuild, and renew. There are moments of joy that light up our paths and challenges that test our resilience. Through it all, I hope these affirmations have reminded you of your own strength, your capacity to love, and your ability to choose positivity no matter what life brings.

This journey of self-discovery, reflection, and growth doesn't end here. Each day is an opportunity to continue shaping your story, to face each sunrise with a sense of hope, and to carry forward the wisdom and resilience you've gathered. Life's beauty lies in its unpredictability and the way it nudges us to adapt, evolve, and stretch beyond what we thought was possible. There will always be lessons to learn, relationships to nurture, and dreams to pursue. We are the lucky ones to still be around to do this, so do it.

Throughout this journey, you've been reminded that growth is not always linear. There will be days filled with joy and motivation, and others that challenge your patience and strength. Yet, through it all, you've shown up for yourself and you will continue to do so. You've practiced self-love, embraced new beginnings, and learned to move forward with grace and courage. Each day brought its own lesson, and together, they've helped you build a stronger, more empowered version of yourself.

I trust that you know, as you walk this journey, your faith can guide you. Trusting in your faith and believing in your destiny is not about knowing all the answers, but knowing you are being guided to where you need to be. Even while being authentic and intentional in your actions, remember there is a higher power leading you, and there is purpose in every step.

Remember, personal growth is a lifelong journey. There will always be new goals to reach, new lessons to learn, and new opportunities to embrace. Be kind to yourself, trust the process, and always believe in your own strength. To believe in your strength or show resilience doesn't mean never feeling pain or ignoring life's hardships. It's about allowing yourself to experience each emotion fully and then choosing how to respond. It's about smiling through your pain, embracing the unknown, and moving forward, knowing that every setback carries within it, the seeds of growth.

You are capable of overcoming any obstacle that stands in your way. The affirmations in this book are reminders. That is all they are—reminders. But the true source of positivity and strength lies within you. You have the power in your hands to create your own **PATH**, **PEACE**, and **PURPOSE**. I do believe that happiness is an inside job. With every breath, every step forward, and every choice you make, you are creating a life that reflects the fullness of who you are. You control your output; you are in control of your emotions. Choose peace.

So as you turn the final page, I hope you feel empowered to live each day with intention, to embrace authenticity, and to trust the journey ahead. Remember, no matter where you are or what challenges arise, you always have the power to **RESET, REFLECT,** and **SMILE** through it all.

Here's to a life lived fully, joyfully, and with an unwavering belief in the beauty of every new beginning.

***

As you step into the next chapter of your life,

- *may you carry with you the wisdom, joy, and resilience you've cultivated over the past year;*
- *may you overcome your fears, pursuing the courage to try;*
- *may you have the audacity to say no and the power of letting go;*
- *may you continue to live each day with purpose, grace, and gratitude;*
- *may you be brave enough to be vulnerable, seeking love in only the right places; and*
- *may you find peace in the present while holding hope for what's yet to come.*

Thank you for taking this journey with me. May it inspire many more to come. Live, love, and laugh. This is not the end.